both feet in the water

both feet in the water

The return of a prodigal daughter

PAT ASSIMAKOPOULOS

CHRISTIAN HERALD BOOKS
Chappaqua, New York 10514

Copyright © 1980 by Pat Assimakopoulos

All rights reserved. No part of this book may be reproduced or transmitted in any form or by any means, electronic or mechanical, including photocopy, recording or any information storage or retrieval system, without prior permission in writing from the publisher.

Christian Herald, independent, evangelical and interdenominational, is dedicated to publishing wholesome, inspirational and religious books for Christian families. "The books you can trust."

ecpa MEMBER OF
EVANGELICAL CHRISTIAN
PUBLISHERS ASSOCIATION

Library of Congress Cataloging in Publication Data

Assimakopoulos, Pat.
   Both feet in the water.

   1. Assimakopoulos, Pat.   2. Christian biography—United States.   I. Title.
BR1725.A82A32   248'.2[B]   79-50943
ISBN 0-915684-31-4

First Edition

CHRISTIAN HERALD BOOKS, 40 Overlook Drive, Chappaqua, New York 10514

Printed in the United States of America

To my husband, Hercules, and my
children, Eliot, Nina, and Eric

Contents

1. At the Edge ... 1
2. The Orphanage ... 9
3. Substitute Parents ... 13
4. A Home? ... 17
5. Search for a Father ... 21
6. You're Just a Guest in This House ... 31
7. Streetwise ... 37
8. Evicted ... 49
9. Black Windows ... 55
10. We Really Care About You—Understand ... 63
11. You're My Little Girl ... 69
12. It's All Coming Unglued ... 75
13. Under Observation ... 79
14. When Can I See My Baby? ... 87
15. Are You Sure You Want to Marry Me? ... 99
16. His Fair Lady ... 113
17. What Happens When the Candy's Gone? ... 123
18. I Want You to Find Someone Else ... 127
19. A Turn For the Worse ... 131
20. A Liberated Woman ... 137
21. If There is Love, it Will Work ... 143
22. Elusive Peace and Rest ... 151
23. Back on the Road Again ... 155
24. Dreams and Visions ... 159
25. I'm Talking About Submission ... 165
26. A Sheep in the Midst of Wolves ... 171
27. Another Lesson ... 177
28. Grace Upon Grace ... 183

1

At the Edge

The three buildings were identical—uninviting cubes of cold red brick. The cab pulled up to the building by the main entrance and stopped. I paid the driver and stepped out. I stood still for a minute and took in the surroundings.

"Do you want me to wait, miss?" the driver said.

"No—I'm sorry—no. Go on."

It was a beautiful day. Fall was at its peak, and the hues of the season flashed their brilliance in the morning sun. I took a deep breath and held it—just to be still, making the moment last.

I was very much aware of the birds singing, rejoicing, I thought. I closed my eyes and whispered, "My God, what am I doing here?" For a moment I wanted to leave, wanted to walk back down the driveway and into town, just forget this whole scheme—this brief venture of courage.

A lot of thoughts edged their way through my mind as I stood before the large double door of the hospital entrance. I had always heard that if you realized you needed help, you had already won half the battle. Well, at least I had done that. But I was only seventeen. What kind of an age is that to be checking yourself into the mental hospital? Was I crazy? Was it just me who couldn't adjust, was it the foster homes, or was it because my mother didn't want me around? What was it? Maybe if I was straight enough to know I needed help, I didn't really need help.

Maybe I was feeling a little sorry for myself, but I didn't care. I just wanted to find out. I didn't know whether this was a step forward or a step back. I had my choice, either to go back to the streets of New York City or check into the state hospital. It was like deciding between two dead ends.

I had been told that if you signed yourself into the hospital, you could sign yourself out. Also, the hospital was free—they couldn't refuse me admission because I couldn't pay. No obligations—the thought was comforting.

The door closed quickly behind me, and the sunshine was gone, replaced by a long, dimly lit corridor. It took nearly a minute for my eyes to adjust to the change in the light. The sound of the birds singing disappeared. I smoothed my clothes, stood up straight, and headed toward the room marked "Admissions."

A drably dressed, matronly woman sat behind the admitting desk. She lowered her head and peered above the rim of her glasses. "May I help you?" she asked.

"I'd like to sign myself in for a while," I answered. The lady motioned me toward the seat in front of her desk. My heart was pounding—I wondered if she could hear it.

"Do you know what kind of hospital this is?" she asked.

"Yes."

"Are you sure you want to do this?"

"Yes, I'm sure."

I answered her quickly. Trying to sound confident and

assured, I continued, "My mother once told me that recognizing your problem is half the battle. I know I need help. I'm an alcoholic and a drug addict. At least I know that much. That's why I'm here."

The clerk turned in her little swivel chair and got up. While she thumbed through a filing cabinet I tried to recall who actually told me that recognizing your problem was half the battle. Was it my mother? One thing was sure—I didn't want to end up in the streets again like a lot of kids I knew. I didn't want to use drugs, I didn't want to drink, and I didn't want to be beaten up anymore. Whatever "normal" was, that's what I wanted.

After gathering up a few papers, the clerk sat down, swung her chair around to face me, and began to fire questions.

"Name?"

"Pat Reich." I didn't want to tell her my real name. She might contact my mother and stepfather.

"Address."

"Bleeker Street, New York City."

"Parents' name?"

"I don't have any—they're dead." I stared down at the paper she filled out. She looked up whenever she asked a question, but I kept my eyes fixed on the paper.

"Any living relatives?"

"No."

"Age?"

"Seventeen."

"Sign here, please." She pointed to a long dotted line at the bottom of the paper. "And here also."

She filled out some more papers and placed them in a folder. She rose from her seat and walked around to the front of her desk. "Follow me," she said. She had a slight smile on her face, but it quickly disappeared.

We walked down one long corridor and then another.

The clerk took a long chain of keys from her pocket and rattled them as we walked up a flight of stairs.

We stopped in front of a door and the clerk began to fumble impatiently with the keys. She looked over her shoulder and glanced at me briefly. *I'll bet she thinks I'm crazy,* I thought.

As I followed the clerk through a large room, a nurse greeted us. The two of them stepped away from me to talk privately. That kind of stuff always frightened me—people talking behind your back and not making any secret about it. What made it worse was that the two of them whispered. When I leaned forward to catch a piece of their conversation, they looked at me kind of funny, backed off a few steps, and continued their talk.

The clerk handed over the folder to the nurse. She patted me on the shoulder, and with an all-knowing, "I told you so" kind of grin, she said "Good-bye, dearie," and headed back the way we had come.

The nurse's eyes quickly scanned the papers in the folder. She gestured for me to follow her. We went to a small room that I took to be the nurses' station. Again more keys. She went inside and placed the folder on her desk. She was so mechanical, so emotionless, as though she were being programmed from somewhere else.

"Am I going to see the doctor now?" I asked.

She said nothing. She turned on her heels and walked down the hall to a large closet. She quickly grabbed a blanket and a garment of some sort.

"Am I going to see a doctor?" I asked again.

"Nope, it's the weekend. None of the doctors work on the weekend. Follow me."

I followed her around a corner into a cavernous, gray-and-white-tiled shower room. Shower heads jutted out from the wall, and drains were scattered around the floor.

"Strip!" the nurse commanded. I looked at her sheepishly.

"Are you deaf?" she bellowed. "I said 'strip.'"

My body ached with fear. I undressed slowly, meticulously, hoping she would turn around and quit staring. But she didn't. Her gaze bore right through me. I felt cheap and degraded. I instantly hated her, and she knew it. It didn't seem to bother her, though. She had probably read the same emotion in the eyes of many patients.

She handed me a gray towel and said, "Take care of it. You won't be getting another one until laundry day next Friday."

I dried, then held the towel in front of me, waiting for more instructions. She leaned against the wall and held out a wrinkled, shapeless smock—she wanted me to walk over and take it from her. Once again I did as she wished.

I was small, and the oversized dress hung clumsily on me. I picked up the towel and my clothes.

"You won't be needing those," she said. She took my clothes from me and picked my pocketbook off the floor.

"Can't I have my comb? It's in my pocketbook. I need it for just a minute."

"Until you get permission from the doctors, you'll have to do without one—some of the patients use them as weapons."

She turned her back and motioned for me to follow her again. Another hall, like a tunnel. We entered a large dormitory room with a long row of beds lined up on each side. The mattresses were thin and gray with black stripes. The small woolen blanket on each cot was black. The place seemed to thrive on dreariness.

"This is your bed." She pointed toward an unused cot near the center of one of the rows. "You are expected to make it every morning before breakfast. Wake-up time for everyone is 5:30. By 6 you must be washed and dressed."

As I made my bed, my eyes clouded with tears. *So this is what happens when someone tries to help himself,* I thought. *At least I can sign myself out.*

I finished the bed. "Follow me," the nurse said again. Weak with frustration, I trailed her down another hall. Her white shoes made a squishing, water-logged sound with each step.

But now there were other sounds—cries, whispers, screams, and frantic talking coming from behind the closed doors we passed. I ran up to one of the doors and peered through a small glass section laced with wire mesh. I saw a woman wearing a straitjacket, mumbling to herself, curled up in a small, thin bed.

I ran to another door and looked in. The room was small. In one of the corners was a young woman squatting, her arms hugging her knees to her chest, her face buried between her knees. I wondered if both these women had arrived in the condition they were in now.

The nurse didn't care if I looked; she just kept walking. We stopped in front of a door that led to another small room. The sign over the door said, MEDICATION STATION. She unlocked a cabinet over a small desk and took down several bottles. After pouring some pills into a paper cup, she handed it to me.

"What's this stuff?" I asked. "I haven't even seen a doctor yet."

"Now, you're not going to give us a hard time, are you?" Her voice had become an irritating whine.

"No, I'll take them. I was just wondering." I was afraid to cry, but I wanted to. But if I did, I might end up in one of those small rooms. I had to please this nurse, even though I hated her. She could make it difficult for me if I gave her any trouble. I followed her down another hall to another large room.

"This is the day room—you'll spend your mornings and afternoons here. You're allowed to go to your bed only in the evening and, with permission, for a short period in the afternoon. Stay in here now. You'll meet the other ladies when they return from lunch."

I stood in the middle of this large room. I had nothing else to do except listen to my thoughts. I didn't like what they were saying. I wrapped my arms around myself and stood tall and rigid. The pain in my chest and stomach was terrible, but I stood straight. I knew that if I bent over I'd be giving in.

My eyes searched the room. I noticed there were iron bars on all the windows. I stiffened even more. My breathing became labored and I started gasping. "Thank God I can sign myself out," I whispered over and over again.

The medication began to take effect. My mouth became dry, and my tongue felt swollen and stuck to the roof of my mouth. I found out later that I had been given Thorazine, a powerful depressant used by mental hospitals to subdue and control their patients.

In about half an hour, the rest of the patients returned. They were led in by a nurse, and they all wore the same kind of shapeless smock I had on. Most of the women I guessed to be around forty. There were a few who were a lot younger and a few who were a lot older.

A young woman approached me and asked, "How'd you get here? You're new, aren't you?"

"Yes."

"Well, how'd you get here?"

"I signed myself in, but I can't wait till I leave. As soon as I see a doctor, I'm going to sign myself out."

A voice from behind me said, "You should have checked with someone who knew better." It was the nurse who had checked me in.

"What are you talking about?"

"You're seventeen, underage, right? You need a parent or guardian to get you out of here."

"But I signed myself in," I protested. "I didn't need a parent or guardian to do that."

"What did you expect us to do, honey, throw you out the front door? You'd have really been mad then."

"But that's ridiculous," I said, breathing very, very carefully and swallowing slowly so all the words would come out right. I went on, yelling that I didn't need anyone to sign anything for me. "I lived on my own in New York City for two years. I had a job and my own apartment. I didn't need anyone to help me—anyone, anyone, anyone. . . ."

My voice trailed off. No one was listening. The nurse had walked away, and the girl who had come up to me didn't even know I was alive. She sat in front of me, stared at the floor, and tried to rock herself in a chair that wouldn't rock.

I got up and went out to one of the balconies off the day room. It was ringed with bars. I grabbed them and tried to shake them loose—so cold. The tears started streaming down my face, and my nose started to run. I wiped it on the shoulder of my dress. Between sobs I screamed at God for what He was doing to me.

2
The Orphanage

My mother held my hand. I was four years old. We stood in the waiting room of a large home. The corridors were filled with the squealing and laughing of small children.

"You're going to like it here," Mom said. "This is a good place."

"Mommy, why can't I stay with you?"

A tall, slender woman came in and led us to a bright, white examination room. "Undress and get on the table," she said. "The doctor will be here in a minute."

The examination was brief. After I finished dressing, the young woman came back and told Mom and me to follow her. I held on tightly to Mom's hand. It was cold, but I didn't want to let go.

"This is the dining hall," the lady said. "We use it for all our meals and to receive visitors. Visiting days are Saturdays." She looked down at me and said, "Say good-bye to your mother. We have to go meet the other children now."

I held on to Mom's neck, sobbing. "Take me with you. Please don't leave. I promise I'll be good."

She unclasped my hands. "This is much more difficult for me. I love you, but you must stay here for a while. You have to be strong and brave. Come on, smile, and let everyone see how brave your are."

"OK, Mommy. Come quick to see me."

"I'll come every weekend, I promise."

I waved good-bye until she disappeared around the corridor. "OK," the woman said. "You come with me now." I held my hand up toward her, but she had already turned and started walking.

The orphanage was run by a robust tyrant named Mr. Campbell. We rarely saw him. It was his job to instill the fear of hell into the children. Mass punishment was meted out often, and for the slightest infraction.

One night I was routed from my sleep by the sound of one of the woman employees screaming.

"All of you downstairs, now! I'll teach you not to make a racket in the middle of the night."

I rubbed my eyes. I didn't know what was happening. I went downstairs with the rest of the children.

"Get in a straight line. Now bend over and put your hands against the wall." We all obeyed. The strap came down hard on each child. When my turn came I stood up before I got hit.

"I didn't do anything. I was sleeping."

"Turn around and take your medicine like the rest or I'll get Mr. Campbell."

"No. I didn't do anything."

"Very well." She nodded to another lady, who quickly left the room. She came back several minutes later, followed by an ominous-looking figure dressed in dark trousers and a black sweater.

"You refuse to take your punishment?"

"I was sleeping. I didn't do anything."

"See this closet over here? I'm going to lock you in it until you remember, and then you'll be punished."

He opened the door and pushed me in. It was a musty

old closet that held brooms, mops, and buckets. I heard a key click the lock shut.

"Little girls who tell lies burn in hell," he shouted through the door. "You just stay there. Maybe by morning you'll remember."

I looked through the keyhole and saw Mr. Campbell and the two attendants walking away. I screamed at them until my throat hurt and my voice cracked. Then I felt along the floor for a space big enough to crawl into. I curled up in the darkness, blinking back the tears. I fell asleep and dreamed of fire all around me.

3

Substitute Parents

My stay in the orphanage was short. From there I was shuttled out to about twenty foster homes. The time spent in each home varied with my ability to cope with a new living situation and the patience of the family I was staying with.

Memories of those foster homes are sketchy—I can only piece some of them together. Most of the pleasant recollections have been blotted out by several incidents that took place in one home in Brooklyn, New York.

Mr. and Mrs. Rodgers had one child, a daughter. The child welfare agency considered them a suitable, well-adjusted couple.

One afternoon, a friend of Mrs. Rodgers brought over some fresh fruit as a gift. The friend said I could have one of the bananas. Without even waiting for me to respond, Mrs. Rodgers asked me, "Aren't you going to give her a big kiss for bringing you that lovely present?"

"Do I have to?" I said. I didn't think it was right to kiss anyone but my real mother.

"Yes. Now give her a kiss and thank her."

"Thank you, but I don't want to kiss you," I said. The friend smiled and waited.

"Well, at least sit down and eat it so she knows you appreciate it."

"Can I eat it later? I'm not hungry now."

"*No!* You'll eat it now!" She grabbed a banana from the table and began to peel it. She tried to cram it into my mouth, but I kept my teeth clenched. She forced my mouth open and began shoving the banana down my throat. After I coughed it up on the floor, she made me pick it up and eat it.

"From now on, because you don't know how to behave in company, you will not be allowed out of your room when we have guests."

Mr. Rodgers and I seldom spoke to each other. He brooded a lot and liked to keep to himself. One afternoon while his wife was gone, he began to talk to me rather hesitantly. "Uh. . . do you like living here?" he asked.

"Yeah, I guess so."

"Then why don't you come over here to the couch and sit next to me?" I did as he suggested. I thought he was just trying to be friendly.

"You're a pretty little girl, Tricia. Would you like me to tickle you?" His voice sounded strange. I started to get up, but he grabbed my wrists and threw me back down onto the sofa. "If I send you away from here," he said, "your mother will never find you. So you better do what I tell you."

He grabbed me by the hair with one hand, and with the other tried to pin my shoulder down. "Now kiss me," he said. His voice was a low, throaty whisper. I couldn't stand his breathing in my face. I began struggling, but an eight-year-old was no match for a grown man. He began to pull me close to him, still keeping a tight grip on my hair.

"I'm going to tell my mother," I screamed. He slapped my mouth hard and told me to shut up.

"Your mother won't believe you," he said. "She'll never come back to get you. Now lie still."

I kept struggling and finally jerked away from his grip. A large clump of hair stayed behind, however. I ran out of the apartment, down the stairs, and into the street. All I kept saying through the tears was, "I want to die, I want to die, I want to die." I ran until I was completely exhausted. I never looked back.

I didn't know where I was, so I began to look around. I saw a tall ladder propped against a telephone pole and remembered that someone had once told me God lives up in the clouds. I ran to the ladder and began climbing. When I got to the top I reached up with both hands. "God, God, please take me with You," I pleaded.

One of the workmen using the ladder ran over and yelled. "Get down from there you stupid kid. You wanna kill yourself?" He had to yell for about five minutes before I'd come down. I hadn't noticed how far I had climbed up and how far away the ground now seemed. Finally, they were able to coax me down.

No sooner did my feet hit the pavement than I was running again. I had to hide. I ended up wandering through the streets for four or five more hours until I finally found my way back. Mrs. Rodgers was furious when she saw me. "Let me handle this," Mr. Rodgers said. He pulled off his belt and dragged me into my room. He closed the door and began flailing at me, not caring where the blows landed. "If you tell anyone I hit you, you're going to wish you were dead." He walked out of the room, leaving me screaming and curled up in a little ball on my bed.

One afternoon I was in my room with the door partially closed. I heard a knock at the front door and Mrs.

Rodgers say, "You know you're supposed to arrange with the agency to visit her."

The other voice was my mother's. It was pleading, "I know, I know. Just let me take her out for a short walk to get some ice cream."

"All right, I guess it can't hurt that much." Then to me she called, "Your mother is here to take you out, Patricia. Go put your shoes on and get ready."

Mom followed me into my room and closed the door. "Hurry," she said. "I'm getting you out of here."

"What? Forever?" I squealed with delight.

"Keep quiet. Don't let her hear you. Come on, get your shoes on fast."

"Can I put on my favorite dress?"

"No, no, I don't want her to suspect anything."

"Can I take my doll?"

"No, I'll get you a better present at Christmas time."

We walked back out into the living room and Mom shouted, "I'll have her back in an hour." We winked at each other as we walked out.

We walked down the street quickly. Neither of us spoke for about five minutes. The suspense was delightful. Finally I asked her where we were going.

"Do you remember the man I was dating, George? Well we just got married, and you're coming to live with us. I'm kidnapping you." She bent down, tweaked my nose playfully, and smiled.

"What's my Christmas present?"

"Well, Santa is going to bring you a brand new baby sister or brother all your own."

"My own? Can I have a sister?"

"I don't know, darling. We'll have to wait and see."

It was all like a fairy tale.

4

A Home?

I never found out if the Rodgers called the authorities. If there was ever any legal problem as a result of what my mother did, I never found out about it.

The first few months of living with my Mom and stepfather were pleasant. They both worked at a restaurant, waiting on tables during the afternoons and evenings, leaving me home to read or listen to music or take walks around the neighborhood.

Around Christmas time, Mom stopped working and came home to await the delivery of the baby—a girl, I knew it would be a girl.

Christmas came and went, and still no baby. Finally, on January 15, Mom went into labor. She called my father at work and told him to come home quickly. Then she went to try and rest. I moved four or five chairs into the room and formed a semicircle around her bed. I sat in one and sat my dolls in the others, and we kept a quiet vigil until my stepfather came and took her to the hospital.

Five days later, Mom was back home with the sister I already knew would be coming. We didn't have a crib for her, so I emptied out one of my small dresser drawers and stuffed it with a soft blanket. We named our little girl Susan.

Susan was not a healthy baby. When she was only a few months old she came down with eczema, a severe skin disorder. She spent her days and nights thrashing around, screaming and trying to tear her skin off. She was hospitalized several times before she was six months old. The doctors wrapped her wrists in gauze and tied her hands down to keep her from ripping at her skin.

The tension in the house taxed everyone's patience. Mom and Dad began fighting, loudly and often. As Susan's condition worsened, the fighting became more frequent.

My responsibility during each evening was to keep Susan from crying and scratching. I would rock her in my arms and sing lullabies to her. I held her close and cried with her. The nights were very, very long.

The conflict between my parents deepened, especially after Mom got a job writing for a Long Island newspaper. My stepfather was still working as a waiter, and it must have bruised his ego to know that his wife was making a larger salary than he was.

Mom drank very heavily. Many evenings she would pass out on the floor. My stepfather and I would put her to bed and set her alarm. We both loved her very much.

Mom talked and wrote a lot about occult practices, spiritism, and reincarnation. She spoke of Bridey Murphy, a woman who, when under hypnosis, could talk for hours of the people she had supposedly been in previous lives. She would revert to those multiple personalities even when she was not under hypnosis. Mom was fascinated by her story, and believed her.

Mom also wrote stories on mind over matter and would practice her research on me. We would sit in the living room of our first home hour after hour, and attempt to move a vase or a chair just through the power of our thought patterns.

Her personality fluctuated wildly. One moment she would flail about in a drunken rage, and the next minute would come over and speak to me quietly, softly, and tenderly. I never knew which person I would meet or have to adjust to.

All the trouble at home had drawn me to the church—at first as a means of escape, nothing more. I could always be certain that from nine to twelve o'clock on Sunday morning the screaming and shouting would be left behind.

By the time I had turned thirteen, I had made many friends in the Methodist church I attended. But one of them, Ruth, stands out most vividly in my memory. She and I went to the same school and spent a few minutes each morning in prayer before we started classes. Ruth would also give me Christian literature: tracts, testimonies, and a few short books. In each testimony it seemed as though God always came to the rescue just in the nick of time. I wondered why He wouldn't rescue me.

My church had decided to take a busload of people to hear Billy Graham speak at Madison Square Garden. There was no shortage of volunteers. I was able to talk to my mother in one of her more sedate moments, and she agreed to let me go on one condition—that I would keep "that Jesus stuff" to myself.

5

Search for a Father

As the opening day of the crusade approached, I became more and more excited. Hearing about God's love from Ruth gave me a warm glow, a feeling of hope. Hearing about it from Dr. Graham would add power.

The Garden was packed. The solos and the hymns were beautiful—I felt as though I was among friends. When Dr. Graham began to speak, I moved to the edge of my seat, waiting to devour each word. After only a few minutes, it was clear that he was speaking just to me and me alone. I forgot about the crowds—he had taken me aside because he knew I was hurting.

I knew he was right. I knew that Jesus was the only answer to the pain I felt. Jesus was the only One who could give me hope.

Dr. Graham gave the call to come forward to all those who wished to receive Jesus as their Savior. "Don't worry," he said. "If you came in a bus, it will wait. Your churches will wait. We have counselors here to speak to you and give you some literature."

I was sobbing as I got up and took that long walk down the stairs to the podium. I continued crying the entire time. I was led gently to a section of the floor where counselors spoke to me about the decision I had just made. I was given a small New Testament. Then the counselor and I prayed together for my growth as a new Christian.

It felt so good.

I was fearful about telling my mother what had happened. It wasn't until two days after the meeting that I mustered up the courage.

"That's OK with me," she said blandly. "Just don't become a fanatic."

The next few weeks I was on a real high. I read my New Testament incessantly and sang out loud all the Christian songs I had ever heard. "Amazing Grace" was my favorite. I prayed constantly—while walking down the street, waiting in the car, during meals, on the school bus, or in a department store.

My most fervent prayers were for my family, because our situation had not changed. It had actually grown a bit worse. Although I tried to be more obedient to my mother, she viewed my new behavior as condescending, a ploy to convert her to my new way of thinking.

Finding my spiritual Father had only increased my desire to find my earthly father. I couldn't talk to Mom about this longing. She forbade it. All I knew about him was his name. I had no address, nor was I sure that he still lived in New York or New Jersey.

I had a plan, a time-consuming one. I drummed up all the telephone books I could and wrote to everyone who had the same last name as my father, hoping that one of the letters would reach him or one of his relatives. The letters looked like this:

Dear Sir:

I hope this doesn't sound strange to you, but I am looking for my father. His name is Pat, just like mine. I was born on April 6, 1943, in Philadelphia, Pennsylvania. My father and mother divorced after he returned from World War II. I have not seen my father since I was a baby. Because your last name is the same as his, I thought you might be a relative. If you know him, would you get in touch with him so I can meet him? Thank you very much.

Pat ———

P.S. He can reach me by writing to the lady whose name and address appear below. She's from the church I go to.

After showing the letters to my friend Mrs. Clark, I mailed them. She told no one in the church what we were doing for fear it would get back to my mother.

The days turned into weeks, and I heard nothing. I had completely given up hope of contacting my father, had even forgotten I had sent the letters, when Mrs. Clark approached me one day after church.

"Come downstairs," she said. "I want to talk to you." We went down into the church basement and sat inside a small Sunday School classroom. Mrs. Clark closed the door behind her.

"Pat, I heard from your father yesterday."

I just stared at her.

"Did you hear me?"

Yes—yes. What did he say?"

"One of the letters you sent reached your grandmother, your father's mother. She lives in New Jersey. She contacted your father and told him about the note. Your father then called me."

"Does he want to see me? Does he want to see me?"

"Yes, he would like to meet you. He wants me to bring you into New York City."

"When, tell me!"

"Well, how about next Saturday. Do you suppose if I

asked your mother she would agree to let you go shopping with me?"

"Oh, I hope so, 'cause I don't ever remember seeing my father."

"We'll try to arrange it," she said, "I'll call your mother tomorrow."

As I walked out the door of the church I was barely able to conceal my excitement. I was walking quietly and serenely, but in my mind I was dancing.

Mrs. Clark called and was easily able to convince Mom to let me go with her. I think Mom was just glad she could get one of the kids out of the house on a Saturday.

I knew that Saturday would never arrive. I spent the whole week staring at clocks at school and at home. I even went to bed earlier than usual because I thought it would make the night go by faster. Every day I set my hair a new way, trying to figure which style would most appeal to my father. I wanted to look mature and sophisticated—if that were possible for a fourteen-year-old to do. I wanted to look so beautiful that he wouldn't want to take his eyes off me. I wanted to look so good that he would ask me to come and live with him.

What would I say? What would he say? I spent nearly every afternoon talking to the bathroom mirror, practicing facial expressions and tilting my head from side to side, wondering which way would look the most "daughter-like." I spoke all the words I hoped would make my father want to whisk me away. "I would help you. Are you married again? I won't get in your way. I'll make you proud of me, I promise."

Suddenly one afternoon I stopped in the middle of my rehearsing. The fantasy was over. All I really wanted to know was why he never got in touch with me. I wanted him to love me and care about me, that's all. I just didn't want him to reject me again. I sat down on the side of the bathtub and cried.

The day finally arrived. I tried on dress after dress, but they all looked bad on me. I felt fat and ugly. I finally settled on a dress I thought was the best of the worst. I looked in the mirror and checked out every angle. Maybe I was trying too hard to make myself lovable. Mom loaned me her good scarf to wear and kept reassuring me that I looked all right.

The drive into the city was exhilarating. Mrs. Clark was enthusiastic and positive that my father would like me. "Pat," she said, "you look lovely. Any father would be proud to have you as his daughter." Her smile was warm and comforting.

We were to meet my father at the Taft Hotel. Mrs. Clark tucked a few loose strands of hair back into my scarf and said, "You just relax and be yourself, sweetheart." She took my hand and led me to the door. A doorman dressed in a black suit with gold brocade and gold buttons opened the door for us. I thought my father must be rich, asking me to meet him at a place like this. Except for a few movies I had never seen a doorman before.

Mrs. Clark went to the registration desk and was gone for about fifteen minutes. I kept looking at all the men going in and out of the lobby, watching for someone who appeared to be looking for someone. As men passed by, my eyes would meet theirs. I wanted to make sure that if my father were looking for me he would have no trouble seeing that I was also looking for him.

Mrs. Clark returned. By her side was a man in his late thirties. He had dark hair, parted neatly on the left. He wore a well-pressed, dark brown suit. "Pat," Mrs. Clark said softly, "this is your father." He walked up and wrapped his arms tightly around me. He lifted me off the floor and kissed me on the cheek.

"Baby, my baby," he said. His eyes were brimming with tears, and I was crying openly. "Boy," he said, "aren't we a sight. Let's stop all this blubbering before they throw us out of this place for disturbing the peace." We all laughed.

"Listen," he said. "I'm going to take you out to a fancy restaurant for a few hours where we can talk—just the two of us. Is that all right with you, Mrs. Clark?"

"Fine with me. I'll meet you back here at 3:30."

My father and I took a cab to a very swanky restaurant. When we walked in the front door he walked over to a waiter, handed him some money, and pointed to the table he wanted.

It was all small talk for a while. We chatted about our health, the weather, and what we were each doing with our lives. I didn't tell him I had become a Christian. Finally the talk got around to some things I really wanted to discuss with him. I asked him why he divorced Mom and why he left. He said, "When I came back from the war, she was going out with someone else."

"Well, then, why didn't you ever visit me when I was in one of those foster homes?"

"Because I never knew where you were. Your mom never told me." He placed his hand over mine and patted it a few times. I believed, or wanted to believe, everything he was saying. The waiter brought our meal.

"I wonder if he thinks you're a young girl friend of mine?" my father said teasingly. "Let's eat our lunch and talk more about this later on."

So this is filet mignon, I thought, *a little round piece of meat that costs a pile of money.*

There were so many feelings, so many questions going

around in my brain. I wanted to ask them all at the same time. The more I thought, the smaller and smaller my appetite got. I ate a few bites and pushed the rest of the meat around the plate with my fork.

I couldn't keep quiet. I told him Mom was a newspaperwoman and that she had become a alcoholic. I told him about school and my sisters and brother, and then, a bit embarrassed, of how I pretended he would sing for me and how we had danced together in my fantasies.

"What about you?" I asked. How many children have you had by this wife?"

"Five, five children. They're all good kids, and they all get good marks in school." He took out his wallet and showed me their pictures. They all looked so happy and well dressed. "They go to a good Catholic school," he said.

"Do they know about me?" I asked expectantly.

"No, they don't. You see, their grandmother is a very strict Catholic. If she knew I had been married before, she would not have let her daughter marry me. So no one knows anything."

"But your wife knows. You knew her before you and Mom divorced."

"Yes, she knows, but her mother lives with us. It's not time to start rocking the boat."

"But why can't you tell them? I mean—maybe I could come live with you." I sat wide-eyed and held my breath, waiting for his answer.

"You know that's not possible. I would do anything in my power to make that happen, but it just can't be, baby." He patted my hand once again. I understood his situation, and yet I believed that if he wanted to, he could change it.

"Look," he went on, "you and I, we'll have our meetings every once in a while. I know it must hurt, but I hurt, too—all these years never knowing where you were or how you were doing."

"But you had to know where I was. You had to sign papers so my stepfather could adopt me. So you had to know. You had to agree, so you had to know. When they found you, why didn't you want to see me?"

"I did, but your mother wouldn't allow it. She threatened to make trouble for my family—so I signed and agreed to everything she wanted."

I didn't believe him, but I wanted him to think I did. I didn't want to lose him or displease him. "It doesn't matter now," I said. "The important thing is that I've finally found you. Is there any way we can write to each other or something?"

"I'd like that, but suppose one of my kids saw a letter of yours. Wouldn't be too good for me, would it?" I was wishing he would be as concerned about me as he was about his new family.

Our time was running out. We had to get back to meet Mrs. Clark. After my father paid the check, we left the restaurant and walked a few blocks, my hand in his. Then suddenly, I pointed up the street and shouted, "Look there's one of those men with a Polaroid camera. Let's have him take a picture of us. Oh please, please!" I was begging. I didn't care anymore about looking sophisticated. "At least let me have one of you if you don't want one of us together." I had never wanted anything so bad.

"Don't be silly, you don't need that." He tugged hard on my arm as we walked quickly past the picture vendor. I didn't want to be a pest, so I didn't ask again, but I ached inside. "By the way," he snapped, "Didn't your mother ever tell you that ladies always wear a hat when they go out?"

"Well, yes, I know. But I don't have one. I'm wearing Mom's good scarf."

"Only peasants wear scarves," he said. "Next time I see you, I want you wearing a pretty hat."

We arrived at the Taft Hotel. My father placed ten dollars in my hand. "You buy yourself something pretty," he said. Then he turned away quickly and walked out the door. Even though I knew he didn't care, I wanted to hang on.

6

You're Just a Guest in This House

"Hi, I'm back," I said.

"So I see." The words were carefully spoken, and my mother's voice was unusually subdued. "How was your *shopping* trip?"

I could feel my face turning red—that embarrassed kind of flush you get when you know you've been caught. "What are you talking about?" I asked.

"Did you find what you were looking for when you went shopping?" Her lips curled up into a sneer and she looked at me contemptuously. "He doesn't want anything to do with you. Yes, he called. You were able to give him just enough to help him twist the knife in me a little more.

Her voice became louder and angrier. "He doesn't love you. Are you blind or just stupid? He has his own family now, and he doesn't want you coming in and lousing everything up. He never wanted anyone interfering in his life—not me, and especially not you. And you, with your big mouth about all my problems, you just gave him the chance to throw some more dirt at me. He made my life miserable for years, years, YEARS! are you listening? Look at me—quit looking at the floor—you're just feeling sorry for yourself.

"And me—besides putting up with all his women I get

the added burden of putting up with you. He never loved you. All those Christmas gifts you got from him weren't from him, they were from me. I signed his name on them to make you feel better. And this is how you go and thank me.

"And you know something else? As far as I'm concerned you can't grow up fast enough to suit me. And while you're in this house you'll tow the line or I'll have you put in a home for wayward girls. And no more church for you, either. If this is what all that religious garbage makes you do. . . . All this Jesus crap is for the birds. I'm sick of it, and I don't want you to mention His name in this house." She turned and walked away, then turned back and shouted, "And another thing. The less conversation you and I have with each other, the better. Anyway, I'm sick of hearing your voice."

I was in no mood to reason. I screamed at her, "I wish you were dead." The waves of hatred I felt were so incredible, they scared me. I screamed those five words over and over again. "I know you hate me. You always had to be someplace else. All the times in those homes when I waited for you to visit and you never showed up.

"You think I'm stupid, don't you. Well you're sick. You lie, you're a drunk—and this is the worst home I've ever lived in. How many of them were there, mother dear? Twenty, or can't you count that high? At least in those places people didn't pretend to love me." I was screaming and crying uncontrollably now—every word I heard was muffled.

"Well," my mother said very calmly. "It just goes to show how ungrateful you are. I made sure you were placed in the best homes. You don't know what I went through for you"—she began spitting out her words—"you little gutter snipe, you little two-cent whore."

"Like mother, like daughter," I said. We both wanted to hurt each other bad. The deeper we could dig, the better.

My sisters and brother became frightened. I put my arms around them and said, "Don't worry, it'll be all right. We were just having a little fight." I was still sobbing, so I don't know if they heard me too well.

My mother ran across the living room and jerked my sisters from me. "You get your hands off them. I don't want them contaminated by you. You just consider yourself a guest in this house from now on and don't step over your boundaries." My little brother ran to my sisters. Mom pulled them all into another room.

I ran to my bedroom, threw myself onto the bed, and sobbed into my pillow. "Why God, why did this happen? I just wanted to see my father. Why is that wrong?" I kept crying loudly and hoped the pillow would stifle the noise. I took the pillow from my face and held it in my arms and rocked myself quietly. My head ached, my stomach ached.

The door to my room was thrown open. Mom walked over to my dresser and grabbed my Bible. "You won't be needing this anymore. You don't even know how to do what it says. You're a little hypocrite."

"Take it," I yelled. "Take it! I don't need it—or you—or anyone!"

Several months later we moved into a beautiful house on Rose Avenue in Floral Park, Long Island. The street was aptly named—everywhere I looked the houses were decked out in roses—red, yellow, pink, and white. I had never seen such a beautiful sight. The trees that lined both sides of the street arched gracefully toward one another.

"This is the result of all the work I've done for you kids," Mom would keep reminding us. "So you can all live right and go to better schools."

Mom and I were going through a truce period. She offered to let me attend the Methodist youth fellowship that met a few blocks from our house. But now that I had the opportunity, I didn't want to go. A change had come over me, subtle but thorough. I wanted nothing to do with anyone, especially Christians. I felt out of place with all the "good kids" who went to the church meetings.

Only one thought kept me going—I was going to find some way to leave home. Even if I was only fifteen, there had to be some way.

As soon as the morning paper was delivered, I would turn straight to the want ads to see if there were any jobs available. I'd find something, maybe a waitress job—anything.

That summer I applied for a job at a restaurant near home. I was told something might open up in a few weeks. Since Mom had once been a waitress, I asked her to show me the correct way to serve. She taught me little tricks, such as balancing a lot of hot plates on your arm without looking silly or unbalanced.

One afternoon I was sitting in an ice cream shop, drinking a soda. I overheard a young man next to me talking to the owner about his job in New York City. After they finished, I asked him, "How do you get to the city from here?"

"Well, do you want to drive—to take the train?"

"Neither—that is, I don't drive. I mean—I'm not old enough, so I guess I mean by bus or subway or whatever."

He swiveled toward me on the stool, put his elbow on the counter, and stuck his fist under his chin. Eyeing me carefully and smiling he said, "You're pretty young—you tryin' to run away?"

"Uh-huh. I want to go to the city and get a job as a waitress till I can find something else."

"Like what?"

"Maybe I could be an actress or something." He sat up ramrod straight and looked around the store to make sure no one else was listening.

"If you're serious," he said, leaning toward me and whispering softly, "I'll help you."

His name was Andy. He was tall and had a sort of olive complexion and a thick frock of curly black hair. He looked like the kind of person I could trust, so I told him all about my life—my age, my circumstances, my parents—everything.

Andy told me which bus to take to get to the "E" train, the train I needed to get to the city. He told me that if I was really serious, he'd meet me at the station at 9:30 the next morning. I couldn't do it then, but the morning after that would be fine. It was the day I was supposed to start summer school to make up some classes I had failed. Everyone would expect me to be gone all day.

Andy said, "I won't wait past ten o'clock. If you're serious, be there by then. By the way, what's your name?"

"Pat."

"How old are you?"

"I was fifteen last April."

"Good. Listen, circle some apartment ads in the paper. Find something you like. Don't worry about where they are, I'll help you find them. How much money do you have? You need rent and security, you know."

"I have about two hundred dollars."

"Well, I guess that's enough to get you started until

you find some work." He got up, grabbed both our checks, and paid the waitress. He was gone before I could thank him.

I waited at the counter a few minutes and then left. On the way back home I walked past the Methodist church. For a moment I was tempted to walk inside and find the pastor. *But what good would he do,* I thought. *He'd probably call Mother. No, that wouldn't work at all.*

I giggled, but I was afraid. I began having second thoughts. The bitterness I felt for Mom had started to weaken, and I would really miss my sister Susan. But it was time to go.

7
Streetwise

With Andy's help I was able to find a large studio apartment on West 88th Street. The rent was $18.50 a week, and I had saved enough money to get me through another month, so I was set. We went to a nearby coffee shop to plan my next move.

I was not exactly street-wise, and Andy knew it. I had left home carrying nothing more than a paper bag full of clothing, a toothbrush, and a comb—not exactly the way for a young sophisticate to start out her new life.

I assumed my mother had put out a missing persons report on me and that I would see my face in all the city newspapers, if not on the front page then at least on the second or third. Andy told me not to assume anything.

He asked me what kind of a job I was looking for. I told him that a waitress job would be fine, but what I really wanted to do was become an actress. When I told him that, his attitude changed quickly. He became very fatherly and told me all about some people he knew in the movie business. He also said he knew a photographer who was looking for magazine models.

"Do you mean magazines like *Seventeen*? That would be nice work," I said.

"Well, not exactly. But you do have a good body, and I'm sure he could find a spot for you somewhere."

I was embarrassed by the way he phrased his statement. "What kinds of magazines are you talking about?"

"Oh, you know, art magazines, that kind of stuff."

"I don't think that sounds like too hot an idea. Maybe I'd be better off looking on my own."

"OK, suit yourself. But if anything comes up, I'm still going to get in touch."

"Fine. See ya around, I guess?"

It was late afternoon, and I felt no motivation to go searching for a job. I sat in my room the rest of the afternoon, afraid to go outside. I knew it would be safer to go out after dark, when no one would be able to recognize me from the picture Mom had put in the papers.

Around eight o'clock I left the apartment and headed toward Broadway. Andy had given me a map of the city, so I had some idea of where I was headed.

I saw a newsstand and approached it with caution. I walked up behind a man, reached around him, and grabbed a copy of *The Daily News.* I tossed my dime on the counter and left quickly. About half a block ahead I saw a policeman walking toward me. I rolled up the paper and put it under my arm. I looked down as I walked, hoping he wouldn't notice me.

When I was sure I was a safe distance from the policeman, I stopped to open the paper. There was nothing about me on the first page and nothing on the second, or third, or fourth, or anywhere. *Perhaps,* I thought, *it will be in the morning edition.*

I loved the feeling of my newly found freedom. I loved being away from the screaming and shouting and drinking and cursing that made living at home so miserable.

I could become what I wanted, not what someone else wanted. I didn't have to answer to anyone. I would make my own breaks. I'd show my mother what her little "guttersnipe" could do. With each step I gained a bit of confidence. By the time I got back to the apartment I felt nearly invincible. First thing in the morning, I'd look for work.

Miss Invincible spent nearly a week wearing out her feet on the New York City sidewalks before she found an exciting job—eight hours a day stamping the backs of checks at an American Express office. Most days were spent trying to keep my eyes open and swallowing potential yawns.

The pay from the job was barely enough to pay my rent and subway fare. Food was a luxury item. Most days, dinner consisted of a slice of pizza and a soda, which cost a grand total of twenty-five cents. In 1958 those were high prices if you were only making thirty-five dollars a week and trying to put away some money to buy a winter coat.

I was able to make friends with one person in my building, an Irish girl named Kathleen. I spent a lot of evenings in her apartment just talking about nothing in particular, trying to revive myself after eight hours of boredom.

One evening Kathleen invited me to go out and have a few drinks with her. I was hesitant and told her I didn't have any identification to prove I was twenty-one. Stretching fifteen by six years seemed an awesome task at that moment. But she assured me I would have no problem getting served.

The bar was only a couple blocks from the building. To gain some instant credibility, I imitated Kathleen's every action. She reached into her pocketbook and pulled out a dollar bill. Then she placed both elbows on the bar and leaned toward the bartender. "I'll have a screwdriver, Johnny," she said.

I pulled a dollar out of my wallet and placed it on the

bar. "Same for me, ah—what did Kathy say your name was? Johnny?" He just grinned and walked away. He came back with two empty glasses and a bottle of vodka. He filled each glass about half full, reached under the counter and pulled out some orange juice, and filled our glasses to the top.

I followed Kathleen's motions and tried to stir my drink just as she did. I was still fearful I'd be found out and laughed right out of the bar. I began sipping the drink, slowly at first, but then a bit more quickly as I became accustomed to the taste. In just a few minutes all the stiffness and fear were gone, replaced by confidence, a relaxed feeling, and perhaps a bit of smugness.

"Two more, Johnny," Kathy yelled down to the end of the bar. "Come on, Pat, drink up before he brings us a refill."

"I don't have a lot of money," I said worriedly.

"That's all right, I'll buy you one. Maybe you can return the favor sometime."

Johnny made our refills, except he made two drinks for each of us. "Why did he do that?" I whispered.

"These extra drinks are from those two guys at the end of the bar." We glanced their way, and they waved at us.

"Who are they?"

"Aw, just a couple of guys who show up here once in a while. Stop worrying. You act as though you've never been in a bar before. Don't embarrass me."

"But they're waving at us."

"So what, have a good time. All they want to do is buy us a few drinks. No one is going to force you to do anything you don't want to."

"What?"

"Oh, come on. Who do you think you're fooling? Just relax, all right?"

The two men came over and Kathleen moved down a

couple of seats so they could sit between us. They began talking and buying us drinks. Gradually the nervousness began to fade; I even got a bit giddy. After I'd finished my fourth or fifth drink I excused myself to go to the ladies room. I walked cautiously and deliberately, trying not to stagger. Once I got into the restroom, I held on tight to the sink so I wouldn't pass out. I stared into the small mirror over the sink and tried to focus my eyes on my reflection. Every move I made seemed grandiose and exaggerated. I sat down on the floor and put my head in my hands, hoping it might help keep the room from spinning any faster than it already was.

I got up and headed back toward the bar. As I sat down I noticed that my drink had been refilled again. "Please," I said. "I don't want any more. I feel really dizzy. Kathleen can we go—Kathy, Kathy. "I looked at the guy next to me. "Where did she go?"

"She left with Danny," he said.

"But where did they go?" He smiled in a way that made me feel very stupid for even asking.

"I have to go," I said. "I have to go to work in the morning."

"Let me walk you home then."

"Sure, if you want to. I only live two blocks from here."

"I know."

"How do you know?"

"Well, Kathy lives there, and you live in the same building, right?"

"Yeah." We walked out of the bar and he grabbed my arm. The fresh air was like a slap in the face. It made me realize again how drunk I was.

When we got to the building he finally let go of me. I stood there on the street, wavering for balance while I tried to locate my apartment key in my handbag. When I finally found it I held it aloft triumphantly. "Here it is," I said loudly, and then I ascended the stairs, slowly, to the front door.

"You sure you don't want a little company?" he said.

"No, I have to get up early. Thanks for walking me home. Maybe I'll see you again."

"Maybe, maybe not."

"Whatever," I said, and shrugged my shoulders.

I had to climb up the staris on my hands and knees to make sure I wouldn't fall. I thought it was funny, and I laughed as I climbed. I sat on the top step and prepared my key for entrance into the apartment door lock. I stood up, pointed my key straight out in front of me, and aimed for the lock. I made it to the door, but bounced off the wall and had to scramble for balance. My second attempt was successful.

I staggered into my room, thought for a moment, then remembered what I had to do. "Set the clock, that's it," I said out loud. I pulled out the alarm button, fell on top of the bed, and passed out.

My next recollection was of a jangling alarm clock and a head that felt as though someone were beating it with a brick. I got up and struggled down the hall to the shower. Even the sound of my footsteps was too loud.

That day, I was glad my job didn't require much thinking. If it had, I would have been in real trouble. Somehow, I was able to muddle through the eight hours.

That evening the hangover was still with me. I was just getting ready to go to bed when Kathleen came over to visit. She asked if I'd like to go down to the bar again.

"I really wish I could, but my head is splitting and I'd really like to get some sleep."

"Don't worry about it," she said. "The best thing for a hangover is a Bloody Mary with lots of tabasco sauce."

"What's a Bloody Mary?"

"Vodka and tomato juice. It'll clear your head in no time at all. Besides, it's Friday. You don't have to go to work tomorrow."

"Yeah, you're right. I'll be ready in a minute."

That evening a friend of Kathleen came into the bar. She was poised, beautiful, and elegantly dressed.

"Who is she?" I asked excitedly.

"Her name's Vicki," Kathleen said.

"Boy, is she beautiful. I wish I could look like that."

"You can. As a matter of fact, you're a lot prettier than her."

"You gotta be kidding. She's a knockout."

"Yeah, but underneath those layers of makeup she's not as pretty as you. I know, because she used to live in our building. One day someone arranged for her to go see this middle-aged woman who runs a house. She taught Vicki how to use makeup, how to dress, how to walk, how to act like a real lady."

"Oh, you mean like a modeling school?"

"No, not like a modeling school. A house, you know—*a house.* You don't know what a house is?" I shrugged my shoulders and shook my head. "A house is a place where four or five girls live—where men come in and pay for their services—to sleep with them—you know, *s-e-x.*" She spelled the word out slowly so it would have more than minor emphasis.

I whispered, "You mean Vicki's a prostitute?"

"Well, yeah, but she doesn't work the house anymore. She stayed a while, but she was able to build up her own clientele, and now she's a call girl."

"What's that?"

"Not much different from a prostitute, except that she has a few select guys that she sees on a regular basis. They pay her lots of money to go out with them. Hey, where have you come from anyhow? I mean, you don't know anything, do you? When you slept with guys, didn't they ever offer to pay you?"

"No—no—I mean, I haven't slept with anyone yet." Immediately after saying the words I was sorry I had said them.

"You're a virgin! Oh, wow!"

"Hey shut up. Don't announce it to the whole world." I was afraid someone would hear and might start laughing.

"Hey, kid, you're valuable merchandise."

"What are you talking about?"

"I bet Vicki knows some men that would pay a lot for a virgin. Bet you could get a thousand, maybe even two thousand. Besides, you could really use the money."

"Are you crazy? I wouldn't do anything like that."

"Why not? Its better than giving it away. If I had your chance, I'd take it. Ah, but it's too late for me," she said with a deliberate sigh. Then she shook her head and laughed. "If only I knew then what I know now"

Vicki came walking toward us from the other end of the bar. "Hey, Vicki," Kathleen said, "I want you to meet a friend of mine. Why don't you have a drink with us? You got time?"

"Just a few minutes. I'm going to the theater tonight. Johnny, give me a Coke, please."

"Since when did you start drinking Cokes?"

"Oh, the man I'm going out with tonight doesn't approve of women drinking. I don't want any liquor on my breath. I'm sorry—what's your friend's name?"

"Vicki, this is Pat. Say, Vicki, I was telling Pat that she could get a thousand or bettter if she's never slept with a guy before."

The blood rushed to my face so fast I thought I would faint. "Kathy, please," I pleaded.

"Look, honey, don't be embarrassed." Vicki patted my

head. "There's always a first time, and if you can turn it to your own benefit, there's no sin in it. What's the difference between someone who gives it away and someone who gets paid? The only difference is that if you're getting paid then you're benefitting along with the guy." She spoke very matter of factly, as if it was some kind of business proposition. "Listen," she continued, "I have to get going." She turned to Kathleen and said, "If Patty decides on anything, give me a call." She turned back and winked at me as she headed toward the door.

"Bye, it was nice meeting you," I said. She had a coolness about her that I thought I admired. I looked at Kathleen and said, "I always thought prostitutes were girls that wore slit skirts, had cigarettes hanging out of their mouths, and leaned against lamp posts. Vicki looks like some rich lady."

"Well, she's got style, but anyone can learn style."

"I bet she could be in the movies."

"Yeah, but she's hoping that one day one of those rich guys she goes out with will ask her to marry him. Then she won't have to sleep with anyone else."

I couldn't get Vicki off my mind. Every time I saw a beautiful woman I wondered if she did what Vicki did. I wanted Vicki to teach me everything she knew about looking pretty, but for my own reasons, not for hers.

I hated my job at American Express. I didn't talk to anyone there and no one talked to me. I began drinking more and more. It loosened me up and helped carry me, although precariously, through each day. I became so used to alcohol that I didn't even get hangovers after a night of heavy drinking.

I had been working for about two months when I came down with what I thought was just a bad cold. For a few weeks all I had was an annoying, hacking cough. I didn't think anything of it. One day, however, while sitting at my desk, I began to get faint and dizzy. I asked my supervisor for permission to go see the nurse. When I stood up to leave, I collapsed. A few ladies rushed from their seats and helped me over to a couch. One of the women ran downstairs and returned with the company nurse. After taking my temperature and pulse, she said it would be best to take me to the hospital.

"I can't afford to go to the hospital," I told her.

"You can't worry about that now. Besides, they can't turn you away. Don't you have any insurance?"

"No, I don't have anything, and I don't want to go to the hospital. I just want to go home." I sat up and leaned my head against the nurse's shoulder. "Please take me home," I whispered. I could barely speak. "I just want to sleep."

"I can't do that, honey," she said as she put her arm around me. "It's my responsibility to take you to the hospital. You don't want me to lose my job, do you?"

"No. I feel fine, though. I just have to sleep. Please take me home."

We walked slowly down to the front entrance, where a car was waiting for us. We arrived at the hospital emergency room and were met by another nurse who sat me in a wheelchair and pushed me inside. I decided not to fight anything since I was growing weaker by the minute. Everything was spinning. I was nauseated and wished I could sleep.

I was brought into the emergency room, where two nurses helped to undress me. I was too weak to fight, to care about my clothes, or anything. I was lifted on to a stretcher, and one of the nurses began to ask questions: name, address, when did I first notice the coughing and so on. The answers came, but it took all the strength I had just to stay awake, so they probably had to ask me several times.

Every few minutes my body would jerk and my eyes would open wide. Every time I looked up it appeared as though there was one more doctor standing there than the time before. I remember hearing snatches of sentences: "Temperature?"

"A hundred and five point two," The voice came from very far away.

I had no control over my body. It jerked and stopped of its own volition. Finally I slept.

8

Evicted

I was told I had pneumonia and would have to remain in the hospital for several weeks. The doctor said it would take me a while to recover fully because I was so malnourished. My resistance was so low that I was extremely vulnerable to infection from the outside. Pizza, soda, and vodka had not exactly been a balanced diet.

The first couple weeks I rested. While I was there I worried—about how to pay the hospital bill, about losing my job, about losing my apartment. I tried calling my landlord several times. He was never around, but I always left him a long message telling him of my situation.

I worried that they wouldn't let me leave the hospital until I paid my bill—I don't know why, but I did. All I had to do, however, was sign the bottom line of a long piece of paper and leave. The clerk at the sign-out desk offered to call me a cab, but I thought the walk would do me good.

The cold air jolted me back to reality the moment I stepped outside. It was a lot colder than when I went into the hospital. The light sweater I had worn then offered little protection against the chill. There was also about an inch of snow on the ground, and I was wearing open-toed sandals. The soles were floppy and paper thin and shoveled up little bits of snow under my toes. After about a block of walking, I was certain they would fall off before I got back to the apartment.

It took me nearly forty minutes to reach my building. When I got there I hurried up the front stairs and into the foyer. I wiped my feet and started to climb the stairs, at the same time waving to the janitor, who was mopping the floor.

"Wait, just wait a minute," he said. "Where do you think you're going?"

I was shivering, and my teeth chattered as I spoke. "I'm going up to my room. Why?"

"That's not your room. You don't live here anymore."

"What do you mean? I do live here."

"Well, you haven't paid your rent, and you haven't been around, so we rented it to someone else just the other day."

"You can't do that. I called you. I left messages. I was in the hospital. You can't do this."

"It's already done, miss. I'm sorry." He walked over to a small closet and pulled out a cardboard box tied up with string. "Here's all your stuff," he said.

"What am I supposed to do? Where am I supposed to go? I don't have another room, and I don't have any money. What about my security? Where is it?"

"It was used for the rent you owed."

"Then I shouldn't owe you anything, and I should still have my room. Either that or my security."

"I'm sorry, miss," he said sternly. "But that's not the way it works. Give me the key, please."

I fumbled around in my handbag and found the key, then handed it to him meekly. "Can I have some of my security back?" I said.

"I wish I could help you, miss. But the answer is still no. I really do wish I could help."

"Yeah, I bet you do," I said angrily as I headed out the front door. "I just bet you do."

I sat on the front steps of the building and searched through my box for something warm to wear. I found a light jacket to go over my sweater. *Now what?* I asked myself. *Now what, bigshot? Now what, Miss Famous Model? You can't do anything. Mom was right. You're a little guttersnipe.* Guttersnipe, guttersnipe—the mocking accusation haunted me. *Here you are on the steps, only a few feet from the gutter. Might as well go sit in it while you're here, make your mother proud of you.*

Finally pushing aside my self-pity long enough to think clearly, I realized I needed to find a place to keep warm. Kathleen wasn't home yet; it was too early. I headed toward Broadway, walking as briskly as I could. The box was awkward and clumsy to carry. I had to switch it from arm to arm every few minutes.

I headed toward the only shelter I knew was available. I opened the door to the bar and was greeted by a welcome blast of warm air. I placed my box on the floor and got up on one of the stools. Johnny came to my end of the bar and put a napkin in front of me.

"Haven't seen you for quite a while. What'll you have?"

"I don't know. How about some advice?"

"Sure. That's why a lot of people come in here. It's cheaper than a psychiatrist, plus you get to have a good time. What's the problem?"

"Well, I've been in the hospital for several weeks getting over pneumonia. I went back to my apartment, and my room had been rented to someone else, and they wouldn't give me back my security, and I only have five dollars and thirty-eight cents left to my name. How's that for starters?"

"What about your job?"

"With my luck, they've probably already hired someone else."

"For one thing," he said, "you need a couple of drinks to straighten you out." He grabbed a bottle of vodka off the shelf and reached for a glass.

"You don't understand," I said. "I don't have any money."

"So what? We'll let you run up a tab. When you start working again you can pay us back." He made a strong screwdriver and set it down in front of me.

"That's good for later, but what am I going to do now?"

"I wish I could take you home, but I don't think my wife would really appreciate it."

"Come on, be serious. I really don't know what to do."

"I know. I'm sorry I don't know what to tell you. Let me ask the boss. Maybe he has an idea or two."

While Johnny was back in the bar's kitchen, talking to his boss, I went to the phone to call American Express. The conversation wasn't long. My job had been taken by someone else. Since it was Friday, I wouldn't be able to go job-hunting until Monday. What would I do until then?

Johnny came back to the bar and refilled my glass. "What did he say?" I asked.

"He told me he would see if there's anything he can do for you. Meanwhile, he told the cook to make you something to eat."

"That's OK, he doesn't have to do that. I can get a slice of pizza somewhere."

"Well, that's the way he is. Don't knock it."

Fifteen minutes later the cook came out with a plate full of steak and onion rings. "What are you giving me this for?" I said. "You didn't have to do this much—go to so much trouble—I mean. . . ."

"Just shut up and eat," said the cook.

I plowed into the food and didn't look up again until the plate was clean. I was so full I couldn't move. "Good job," Johnny said. "You did pretty good for someone who wasn't hungry."

"I didn't know I had so much room," I said. "I'm going to call again and see if Kathy's home."

She had just walked in her door when I called, and she said she'd be right over. As soon as she arrived, I blurted out the whole story as fast as I could. She told me I could stay with her and could go to the restaurant she worked in to check if they had any waitress openings.

I wanted to go back to her place and go to sleep, but I didn't want to force her to leave. It was Friday night, and I knew how much she looked forward to that.

One of her boyfriends walked in around eleven o'clock and started making small talk with her. I felt like excess baggage, so I left their booth and walked back up to the bar. Johnny kept giving me drinks and handed me a roll of quarters that I could use to play the jukebox. The quarters were all marked with a dab of red nail polish. Johnny said that was because the people who installed the machine would give the bar back all the money they put in, so the money was marked to keep it separate.

After returning from one of my trips to the jukebox, Johnny asked, "Where's your friend?"

I looked around. "Maybe she's in the ladies' room." I went back to check, but I couldn't find her.

"I was pretty sure she wasn't in there," Johnny said. "The guy she was talking to paid her bill and his own just a few minutes ago."

"Why did she leave me? How could she leave me stranded like this?" I looked up at the rotating clock over the bar, waiting for the beer sign to turn around and expose the time. It was 2:30 in the morning. The bar would be closing at four. While I was sipping on another drink, wondering what to do, the owner came over to my seat.

"Johnny told me what happened. Here, here's forty dollars to get you through the weekend. You can get a hotel room up around 95th Street or maybe even something on Amsterdam Avenue. But if I were you, I'd try to stick to Broadway, especially at this time of night."

"Why are you doing this?" I asked.

"Hey, everybody gets into a tight spot sometime. Don't worry about it. Pay me back when you can, and during the weekend you can come in here to eat."

I took the money from his hand carefully. "I'll pay you back as soon as I can, I promise. I will."

"Good. Now let me get you a cup of coffee to warm you up."

He went back into the kitchen and came back out with the coffee. I sipped it for a long time, staring down at the bar and thinking, trying to put all the pieces together.

9
Black Windows

The job hunting was not easy, but I was finally able to land a job as a barmaid from six at night till four in the morning. Nobody asked about my age, because nobody cared. Every time someone ordered a drink I had never heard of, I looked at a chart I had taped to the wall at one edge of the bar. No one ever knew.

I wanted to use the job as a stepping stone to find another one. I certainly didn't want to tend bar for the rest of my life. Inhaling smoke and alcohol fumes ten hours a day was not my idea of fulfillment.

I was able to find another apartment quickly, a better one than I had had before. It was twenty-five dollars a week, and the landlord wanted only one week's security. The tips I made at the bar were good, and I was able to pay the rent without much of a problem.

The first order of business, however, was to pay back Johnny's boss and disengage myself from that crowd. They were decent people for the most part, but there was something about them I didn't trust. They were generous, but I always felt uneasy around them. I felt as though I were a Yo-Yo; as long as they could run up a tab for me they would keep me on their string. I didn't like that kind of dependency.

Foolishness, however, will often win out over logic in

the mind of a sixteen-year-old. My fantasies for my future were pretty high-flown. I was always a top business executive or a *Vogue* magazine fashion model. I was always drawing the adulation of the crowds. Photographers and reporters shoved each other around, each of them hoping to get an exclusive interview or an exclusive shot. I was also paying periodic, imaginary visits to my mother to let her know how well I was doing.

One afternoon on my day off, I ran across an ad that looked as though it had fantasy possibilities. It was for a cigarette girl at a night club in New York City's Latin Quarter section. The hourly wage was low, but the ad guaranteed good tips.

My image of the typical cigarette girl came from B-grade movies on the late show—short dresses, black knit stockings, and long, jet-black hair. I stood in front of my mirror and attempted to strike a cigarette-girl pose. I walked across the room toward the mirror, exaggerating each step and practicing my lines: "Cigars, cigarettes, cigars, cigarettes? What brand, sir? Of course, here you are." I reached out my empty hand to my imaginary customer. "And your change, sir. Oh, thank you very much, sir," I said, and discreetly deposited the dollar tip.

I threw on my coat and ran out to the nearest department store. I bought black stockings with lines up the back and little black stars knit on them. I went to another store and bought a black, form-fitting dress, spiked heels, and black hair rinse.

When I got home I combed the rinse through my hair and put it up in curlers. When I took them out my hair was pitch black, with a few brown roots visible if you stared long enough. I put on the stockings, the dress, and the spiked heels. I put on my makeup, putting some extra emphasis on the black eye liner. For a final touch I put on fire-engine-red lipstick.

Pulling one side of my hair in back of my ear, I fastened the hair in place with a pin. I stood in front of the mirror and saw that I had been transformed into a woman of the world. I moved back to the rear of the room and took in the full effect as I walked toward the mirror once again—"Cigars, cigarettes."

I had to catch two different buses to get to the Latin Quarter. Wearing the outfit I was wearing, I'm amazed that I wasn't arrested or propositioned.

When I got to the nightclub, I found that the cigarette-girl job had been filled, but that they had another position open for a hat-check girl.

The woman in charge of personnel at the club told me I could have the job if I wanted it. "Try it out," she said. "If it doesn't fit, quit and we'll get someone else."

"What do I have to do?"

"Just take the coats from the people as they come in, and put them on a hanger. Then give them half of one of these tickets. Got it?"

"Sure."

"Oh, there's one thing you've got to remember. This is a concession. That means that all the tips belong to the concession owners. Most tips are dollar bills or better. You don't know who will be handing you the money. It may be someone the concession owner has hired. The money may also be marked—the serial numbers could be written down somewhere, and the boss will check them off at the end of the day. If some are missing, it means you pocketed it. That means you're in trouble."

"Fine, but how do you make any money if you can't keep the tips?"

"Come on, honey, you look like you've been around. If a girl wants to make extra money, she can find a way. Just keep your hands off the tips. Oh, another thing—smile, smile, smile. No matter what the customer says to you, smile. These people pay a lot of money to have a good time here, and we want them leaving in high spirits. Understand?"

"Yeah, I got it." The whole evening I had my phony smile glued on. My face began to hurt from smiling too much. At the end of the evening, the woman I had talked to earlier said, "Well, are you going to stay, or shall we look for someone else?"

"Maybe you'd better look for someone else. I can't make any money here. It doesn't make sense. Besides that, it's boring. I guess I'll go back to my other job." The next evening I was back behind the bar again, minus the costume and the black hair rinse.

Working at the bar got to be a pretty comfortable job. We didn't cater to rowdy people, so the place was fairly quiet. The tips got better as some of the regular customers got to know me.

One Saturday morning, after getting home from work and showering, I decided to take a long walk down to Greenwich Village and rent a bicycle. I walked for seventy-eight blocks, looking in store windows and watching the people.

The bike ride was beautiful. The breeze trailed my hair out in back of me as I whisked through the Village, heading for the financial section of town. I rode right down the middle of Wall Street, which was absolutely deserted. I turned in and out of one narrow street after another, singing and laughing. I made believe that I was the only person left in a huge, abandoned city. I shouted and yelled and listened as my voice echoed off the walls and down the streets.

I rode up to a large Episcopal church, parked the bike, and went up to the door, but it was locked. I was annoyed. I wondered what possible reasons a church could have for keeping its doors locked.

I rode around some more until I reached the Staten Island ferry. I crossed over and rode around the island, stopping for a few minutes to have lunch. Then I took the ferry back to the city and rode back to Greenwich Village. I went to a coffee house and ordered a cup of coffee. I looked around at all the people, so different from those in my neighborhood, playing chess and backgammon and drinking espresso. Other people were sitting at tables, reciting poetry to one another. The people sitting at the table behind me were discussing religion and politics. I liked it a lot and made a mental note that I would have to return soon.

It was getting dark, and I thought it would be best to take a cab back home. I decided, however, that I'd like to have a drink before the ride back. So I stopped at the first bar I passed and ordered a screwdriver.

While the bartender was making the drink, two big men walked up and stood beside me. One of them stared down at me and said, "My my, what do we have here?"

I turned and faced him. "Look, mister, I just came here to have a drink, and then I'm leaving. I'm not looking to get picked up, so please leave me alone."

The other man handed me my drink. "Here you are, young lady. Hey," he said to his friend, "leave her alone and let her drink in peace." They both walked down to the end of the bar, but in a few minutes they were giggling like a couple of schoolgirls. *Just imagine,* I thought, *guys their age acting like children.*

I don't remember finishing it. The next thing I do remember I was sitting on the edge of a bed in a strange room. One bare lightbulb hung by a shredded cord in the center of the room. There was no other furniture in the room, and the glass in the window had been painted black. I held the small, grayish sheet to my body and started to cry. The door to the room was open, and I cried out loudly, "Where am I? What happened to me?"

I looked around the room for my clothes, but I couldn't see them anywhere. The crying stopped and panic took over. I staggered to the door with the sheet wrapped around my body and walked down the hall until I found another room. It looked like the one I had just come from. I walked in and began searching. I found my clothes rolled up into a ball in the corner of the room. A sleeve had been ripped off my blouse, and the zipper and button had been torn off my pants. As I dressed I began crying again. I didn't know if it was night or day. All my things weren't in the corner—I still couldn't find my pocketbook, my jacket, or my shoes. I headed back into the other room and found my shoes and jacket under the bed. I put on my jacket and held my shoes in my hand so I wouldn't be heard as I tried to get out of the building.

I quickly and quietly ran down the stairs. I heard voices coming from another part of the building, and that made me hurry even more.

As I opened the door to the street, an alarm sounded. I panicked and ran as fast as I could, not caring about which direction as long as it would take me away from that building. I didn't want to be grabbed and thrown back inside.

My body ached, but the fear I felt was greater than the pain. My legs were moving faster than my ability to control them, and I stumbled several times. As I got farther and farther from the building I looked around, trying to figure out quickly where I was. I saw a lot of ships and trucks—I was along the docks. The buildings around me were mostly old and abandoned, with many broken windows.

More pain tore through my side as I ran faster and faster. As I approached a fairly busy intersection I slowed down, then stopped to put my shoes on. I tried to gain control of my breathing. *I can't go to the police,* I thought. *I can't do anything.*

I reached into my pocket to see if I had any money, and with a sigh of relief I discovered that I had a little more than I needed for a subway ride home. I ran down the stairs of the nearest subway station and bought a token. Just as I slipped through the turnstyle, a northbound train pulled in. I ran into the train as fast as I could, barely missing being clipped by the mechanical doors as they closed quickly behind me.

The subway rocked me back and forth. It had a soothing effect, and I was able to calm down just long enough for the humiliation and shame to hit me full force. I began to shake as I imagined what had happened to me. I felt like a piece of trash someone had tossed into a gutter.

10

We Really Care About You—Understand?

I ran into my bathroom and undressed quickly. My right eye was swollen and both cheeks had been badly bruised. I looked into the mirror and screamed, "You're no good for anyone now!" I stepped into the shower and let the warm water run over me for a long time, washing away the tears.

But no matter how long I stayed under the water, I didn't feel clean. I washed myself, gently, over and over again. Even the slightest pressure created more pain. I couldn't get clean.

I stepped out of the shower and looked at my face in the bathroom mirror. "You've got to go to work," I said.

"No, I can't. It hurts too much."

"You have to be brave."

"No I don't."

"No one is going to take care of you. You have to be brave."

"I do not!"

"Why don't you just go home, then?"

"No, I'll never go home."

"Then you'd better go to work."

It was two-thirty in the afternoon. I had to be at work at six. I couldn't even figure out how long I'd been away. Maybe I'd already missed a day of work.

I set my clock for five and went to bed. After what seemed like an eternity, the alarm went off. I woke up and found that I was curled up into a ball and sucking my thumb, something I hadn't done for years. I got up, dressed, and went to work. For the first time I felt fear as I walked the streets, fear and hatred and bitterness and dirtiness.

One morning after returning from work, I was especially tired and went right to bed. Actually, I was drunk. I had started letting the customers at work buy me drinks. Most mornings I passed out and slept until it was time to leave for the bar again.

So far, this morning had been no different. I had drawn the blinds, and the room was still. I closed my eyes and started to drowse. Suddenly I sat up, just in time to see a sheepdog running across my room. As I stared at him, watching him prance back and forth, I noticed something strange—he was transparent. Then a little man, the same size as the dog, came in and ran across the room several times more.

My God, I thought, *I'm seeing things.* I had the D.T.'s—that's what Mom had. She would pace across a room, seeing things we couldn't see and talking to people we couldn't hear. The D.T.'s; that's one step beyond alcoholism. I was drinking so much that the alcohol was doing more than just acting as a depressant. It had become an hallucinogen.

I talked to the dog and the man. I told them I wasn't afraid of them, that if I closed my eyes they would go away.

The D.T.'s continued on an irregular basis. Sometimes I would see my mother with two other ladies, and sometimes she would be talking with the dog. I could see their lips moving, but I couldn't hear what they were saying.

I wanted to get in touch with my mother and sisters and brother. I know what Mom would say if I told her I was a barmaid. That would be the end of the conversation, and I might not get another chance to see her or the rest of my family ever again. So I had to go look for another job, a more respectable one.

After applying at several large restaurants in the city, I saw an ad for a waitress at a little luncheonette in Forest Hills, Queens called The Penguin. I walked in during the peak of the lunch-hour rush and went to the back of the luncheonette, just to look around.

A lady sitting at the end of the counter asked, "How's the pastrami today, Leo?"

"Lean, nice and lean."

At the end of the counter, next to a meat-slicing machine, was a customer receipt book. I grabbed it, walked up to a table that hadn't been served yet, and took the order. "Three briskets on a roll, hold the sauce. Two hamburgers on one plate with a side of fries," I shouted over to Leo.

"Two hamburgers on one plate are called burgers twenty-one," Leo said.

There was no stopping me. I took orders as fast as I could until the end of the rush. At two thirty, Leo called me over to one of the booths and told me to sit down.

"What's your name?" he asked.

"Pat."

"Pat, you did a good job today. You looking for work?"

"Yes, I am."

"You got it."

"Really? Thanks, I need a job."

"You're not working now?"

"I'm working, but I don't like my job."

"What are you doing?"

"I work as a barmaid at night."

"How old are you? Have you left home?"

"Why do you want to know?"

"Listen. I've seen all kinds of kids come through that door over there. I don't know why so many runaways end up here, but they do. I end up nursing kids, off and on, from all over the place. You don't have to worry about me. As long as you work hard and keep your nose clean, you can have a job here. Phyllis and I will do anything we can to help you."

"Who's Phyllis? Is she your wife?"

"No, she's been working here for fifteen years. We've seen a lot of kids come and go. Some make it, some don't."

"But how did you know about me, that I was a runaway? I've been living in the city for quite a while now. No one ever asked my age, even when I applied to work as a barmaid."

"Why should they? Besides, they're probably paying off the cops anyway."

"How do you know all these things?"

"He knows a lot more than you think, honey," one woman said as she walked by our booth.

"How old are you? Sixteen? Seventeen?" Leo asked.

"Yeah, about that."

"Well, listen. If you want to make it, it's up to you. Work hard, and stay away from the kinds of people that can pull you down. By the way, my name is Leo, Leo Kaufman. That was Phyllis who walked by our table just a minute ago. If you want to work, the hours are from six in the morning till five in the afternoon. Go out and buy yourself a white uniform and some white shoes, nurse's shoes. Otherwise your feet will kill you all day long."

"Do you want me to finish out today?"

"No, come in tomorrow. Get things straightened out at your other job. I'll see you in the morning."

Leo and Phyllis became closer to me than my own family. Leo always seemed to know my moods and what was going on in my mind. I talked to him about everything, especially about my desire to see my father again. He didn't encourage me too much because he was afraid I would be in for a big letdown.

Leo was very protective of me. He kept a close watch on the guys I would date and the kind of people I spent my time with. Leo's stamp of approval meant a lot. Often, however, I would go around with people Leo didn't approve of. He never got too upset but warned me about the kind of trench I might be digging for myself if I continued to keep unsavory company.

One of my new friends had introduced me to the euphoric feeling of getting high on marijuana. One evening we smoked a couple of joints, losing all sense of time. When I suddenly discovered that I had to be at work in an hour, my friend offered me some Benzedrine (bennies). I was wide awake and alert within ten minutes.

Leo was never fooled. He knew I was on something. "What have you been taking, Pat?" he asked as soon as I got to work.

"What do you mean?"

"Hey, baby, I'm not stupid. Don't try to play games with me. You been smoking dope?"

"I just tried it. It wasn't much."

"You know that girl you're hanging around with is a pusher."

"She didn't sell me anything. She gave it to me."

"She'll give it to you for a while. She'll sell it to you later. What else did she give you?"

"I took a benny. I couldn't get started this morning. I just thought I'd try it."

"Everyone thinks they're *just* going to try that stuff. I've seen too many kids messed up on that junk. I don't want to watch you do it, too."

"I'm sorry. I didn't mean to disappoint you and Phyllis."

"The only reason we're disappointed is that all you're doing is hurting yourself. We don't want you to have to finally learn your lesson when the bottom falls out and you have no other choice but to learn. You understand? We really care about you. OK?"

"OK."

"Good. Now hurry up and get to work or we won't be ready when the customers get here."

11
You're My Little Girl

I ran into the luncheonette as fast as I could. "Leo, Leo, guess what, guess what?"

"Calm down and talk slowly. Now what happened?"

"I called my father last night, my real father. Remember I told you about him when I wrote all those letters to try and find him?"

"Yes, what about him?"

"He's agreed to see me. This Saturday he has to travel to New Jersey on business. He said he would take me with him so we can get to talk and to know each other better. Isn't that great?"

"Saturday?"

"Yes. Do you think I could have the day off?"

"Sure, anytime. But listen, I don't want to throw cold water on your enthusiasm, but don't get your hopes up about anything. He can't be that great a guy or he would have helped to take care of you. I've seen situations like this before. I just don't want you to get hurt."

"Oh, Leo, I know. Don't worry." I put my arms around him and kissed him on the cheek.

That evening I went shopping for a dress to wear on Saturday. Then I remembered how much he loved hats, so I went to look at those first.

I tried on hat after hat until I finally found one I liked. It was a nice straw hat decorated with tiny pink flowers. I chose a light blue dress to go with it. A white pocket book, white high-heeled shoes, and white gloves topped off what I thought would be a perfect outfit. Now my father would have to take me back.

I didn't sleep much Friday night. I was nervous, but I also had a head full of curlers and rollers that added to the problem. About a hour before he arrived, I bathed and dressed myself meticulously. I wanted to be perfect, not like the little baby he had seen the last time.

I fluffed up the pillows on my couch and opened the windows to let in some fresh air. I was proud of my apartment and wanted it to look nice for him. I put on a fresh pot of coffee, because I knew he liked it.

The doorbell rang. I pressed the buzzer to open the door downstairs, then ran back to the mirror to make sure my hair was in place. Then I dashed to the door just in time to answer the knock.

"Don't you have an intercom?" he asked.

"Yes, but I knew it was you."

"Never mind. You should use it; you never know."

He walked in and began looking around. I waited for him to say something. "Do you smell the coffee?" I finally asked. "I made you a fresh pot. I know you must be tired after driving all the way from Brooklyn."

"No, we don't have time for that. I have to get to New Jersey. We'll have to leave right away."

"Not even time for one cup?"

"No, sweetie, we have to go."

"OK, let me get my hat and gloves." I reached up into my closet for my hat and set it carefully on my head. "How do I look?"

"You don't look sixteen, that's for sure."

"I'm not. I just turned seventeen," I said proudly.

"You don't look seventeen, either," he said, as he took my arm and guided me out of the door.

"Is that good or bad?"

"It can be either."

"How do *you* mean it?"

"Well, I guess you could say you look gorgeous—ravishing, as a matter of fact."

"Good. I wanted to make you happy. I bought this whole new outfit just for you."

We walked two blocks to where he had parked his car.

"Boy, this is a big car," I said when we got there. "Is it yours?"

"Of course it's mine." He opened the the door, took my arm, and guided me gently into the front seat. I was so thrilled that he was looking after me.

After we had been driving for a few minutes, he said, "Tell me about yourself. Why did you leaave home?"

"Oh, come on. You know why I left home. The last time I saw you I trusted you not to call mother and tell her we had gotten together. But you called her anyway. This time, please don't tell her where I am. I'm doing fine. I have a nice job as a waitress, and sometimes I go out on catering jobs with my boss. I have close to a thousand dollars saved up."

"You should go to school and learn how to type and take shorthand."

"Maybe one day. But I'm doing much too well now to be thinking about school. How about you? How are your kids doing?"

"Oh, fine. They all still go to a Catholic school. My oldest son wants to become a doctor. Did I show you a picture of them?"

"I think I saw one the last time I saw you."

"Well here, take a look," he said, handing me his wallet opened to a picture.

"The children are beautiful. Is this your wife?" I pointed to a redheaded woman in the picture.

"Yes, it is."

"Wow, is she beautiful!"

"She was once a contestant in a Miss America contest."

"I know this sounds ridiculous, but I feel jealous of your children and your wife."

"You're right. It is ridiculous. Now listen. When we get to the town I have business in, I'm going to rent two motel rooms, because I might have to spend the night there. I'll rent the rooms and then drop you off at the shopping center while I take care of business. Then we'll have a late lunch and a nice talk. I'll take you back to the motel and you can watch television, and I'll go out for my next appointment. Then we'll have dinner together."

"That sounds like fun."

We drove into a small town in New Jersey and pulled up in front of a nice motel. "This isn't too far from where I have to work," he said. "Let's see if they have a couple of rooms." I started to get out of the car. "No, you wait here," he said. "No sense in both of us going."

He came back in about ten minutes. "We're lucky," he said. "They had two rooms, and they're connecting rooms, so we won't be too far from each other. Now let's get out to that shopping center."

We pulled up to the main entrance of a large shopping center. Dad got out his wallet and handed me some money. "Here, get yourself something pretty. Meet me back here in a couple of hours."

The shopping center bored me. I wanted my father to hurry back. He was late, and I had to wait an extra hour. Finally, he pulled up to the entrance and jumped out of the car. "Sorry I'm late, sweetie. I couldn't help it. You forgive your daddy?"

"Of course I forgive you. It doesn't matter."

He took me to a beautiful Italian restaurant and ordered in Italian just to impress me. The waiter left and in a few minutes brought over a bottle of wine. I leaned over and whispered, "I didn't know you could speak Italian."

"I'm full of surprises," he said as he held up his glass of wine in a toast. "To my little girl." He clicked his glass against mine. "I'm going to make it all up to you. I promise I will; all those years we didn't spend together—I promise."

After lunch (it was actually closer to dinner time), he took me back to the motel. He had to go out on one more appointment. He promised he would be back by eight o'clock.

Alone in the motel room, I savored all the happiness I had had in one day. My father was pleased with me. I walked over to the mirror and took off my hat. I took off my dress and hung it up so it wouldn't get wrinkled. I got into bed, pulled the blanket over me, and sat up to watch television. I hadn't watched television since I'd been back at my mother's home.

"Wake up, sleepy head." It was my father.

"Hi—what time is it? I must have dozed off."

"I got back a little early. It's just a quarter to eight."

"Look," I said, pointing to my dress on the hanger. "I didn't get it wrinkled."

"Good girl. Let me ask you a question. Why do you wear your hair up like that?"

"Don't you like it? I think it makes me look older."

"I don't know. I haven't seen it down. Why don't you take the pins out? Turn around, I'll do it for you. Where's your brush?" he asked.

"In my pocketbook."

"When my other little girl was younger, I used to comb her hair. I never had a chance to comb yours. I'll do it now."

"This is unreal," I said excitedly. "I can't ever remember anyone brushing my hair for me."

"You look beautiful," he said. "Let me hold you."

For a moment I was frightened. But then he said, "Hey, I'm your father. I'm not going to hurt you. Let me turn you around and take a look at you."

I turned around. "I think I better put my dress on," I said, "I feel silly sitting here like this."

"You don't have to worry. I've seen a lot of women in their slips. You're my little girl. I just want to hold you, OK?" He got on his knees on the bed and put his arms around me. "See. I just want to hold you. Don't be afraid. I'm your father."

I wasn't sure how to react. One voice inside me said, *He's your father, dummy. He loves you.* Another voice said, *If he loved you, he wouldn't hold you this way.*

"Please, don't—if you love me—don't!" I said.

"I do love you, I do love you."

My lips curled in disgust as I saw him getting ready to leave in the corner of the room. He walked out the door, and it wasn't long before I heard his car start.

12
It's All Coming Unglued

"Hey, it's only five o'clock," Leo said as he walked in the door. "What are you doing here so early?"

"I couldn't sleep well, so I thought I'd come over."

"So tell me, how was your visit with your father?"

"I really don't want to talk about it."

"Yes you do, that's why you got here early. Come on and we'll talk for a while. I'll go make us some coffee."

I sat down at a corner booth. As soon as Leo sat down, I began crying and blurting out the entire story, down to the last detail.

"It's an old story, Pat. It's happened to a lot of girls. The girl who worked here before you was also raped by her father. Unfortunately, it's not that uncommon.

"Look, the guy's a bum. Maybe a bum who dresses in expensive clothes, but still a bum. The important thing is that you don't go around the rest of your life feeling guilty about something he did. If you don't rise above it, the memory of what happened can eat you up, devour you. You understand me?"

"Yeah, I guess. But if he loved me he wouldn't have done that."

"That's right. Now what you have to do is accept the fact that he doesn't love you. You can't win the love of someone like that. He's a user, baby. He uses people. He used your mother. He used a lot of people. He's been married five or six times, hasn't he?"

"Yes."

"Well, that should tell you something about him. Let me go get you some coffee."

I lit a cigarette. Leo came back to the table, put down two cups of coffee, and wiped my tears with a napkin. "Look," he said. "This isn't much, but Phyllis and I love you. This is your little family here. But I want to warn you that how you react to things now is very important. You musn't let this thing pull you down. I know that doesn't make you feel any better now, but I don't want you to forget what I'm saying."

I put my head down on the table and cried as hard as I had ever cried before. "That's OK," Leo said, "have a good cry. Have a good cry. You need it. Everything will be OK."

But everything was not OK. Everything did not get better. All the assurances in the world couldn't convince me that I wasn't the little two-bit whore my mother thought I was. The guilt was crushing. I couldn't shake the thought that I had in some way provoked my father, that somehow I had encouraged him.

I had always dreamed of getting married, of having a husband who would love and care for me as I would for him. But now, I thought, that would be impossible. No man would take a woman like me—ever. I wanted sex to be beautiful and to be enjoyed for the first time with the man I would marry. I thought that's what God wanted, not having my first two sexual experiences being rape and then incestuous rape. What kind of God would allow that to happen to one of His people? What kind of God would allow someone to be degraded and cheapened by her own father? All I knew was that I was alone, and I was ashamed, and God was far away. If this was the way He loved and cared for His creation, I wanted no part of it.

Alcohol and pills became my way of hanging on, my way of coping with the shame. Leo's periodic pep talks were helpful, but they didn't ease the emptiness, the meaninglessness of my life. The talks would ease my mind for a few minutes, the pills and alcohol for several hours, or even a whole evening.

I was coming unglued, and there was nothing I could do about it. It was not a peaceful feeling, but neither did I fight it. I claimed no more responsibility for my life. I was numbed; no one could do anything that would surprise me.

One evening the hallucinations began again. I closed my eyes and put my pillow over my head, anything to get rid of them. But they haunted me all that evening and wouldn't go away. I had to get help.

One afternoon on my day off from work, I called Leo. I had made a decision.

"Leo, I have to go away—to a state hospital or something."

"Why a hospital?"

"Leo, it's all falling apart. I can't hold it together anymore. Right now I want to go. If I wait, I may not want to. Do you understand?"

"I'm listening. Talk to me."

"I want to sign myself into a state hospital. They have psychiatrists there. I need to get away, to get things straight in my mind."

"There are other ways, Pat. That may not be the solution for you. Have you thought of a private psychiatrist?"

"You know I can't afford that. I don't think I have a choice. Don't you understand?" I began to sob. "Leo, are you there?"

"Yeah, baby, I'm here."

"Leo, I can't hold it together. I don't think I can make it unless I do something now."

"OK, whatever you say. Why don't you come over here so we can talk a bit."

Within the hour, I was at the luncheonette, suitcase in hand. "You've really decided, haven't you?" Leo said.

"Yup, this is it."

"You want to have some breakfast together before you leave?"

We sat quietly during our meal. There wasn't much to say. Leo made a few light attempts to dissuade me, but they didn't work. "Here, honey, take a few cartons of cigarettes with you," he said when he had finally given up trying to talk to me out of my plan. "Write to me. If there's anything you need, you know I'm always here.

13

Under Observation

The morning alarm at the hospital was not polite —a loud buzzer accompanied by lights being switched on and off. It was still dark outside. I automatically dressed and made my bed, remembering what the nurse had said the night before. I intended to be self-sufficient and not give anyone any trouble.

As soon as we were dressed, the line formed at the medication station—more Thorazine. I wondered how long it would be before I'd get to see a doctor, how long it would be before I'd get to see my family. They didn't even know where I was. *You warned me Leo, you warned me. Warned me about my father and warned me about this. I should have listened to you.* I wanted to scream at someone, but I couldn't show anyone that I wasn't in control.

Every day at the hospital was like the one before: wake up, medication, eat, showers, medication, eat lunch, sit around, medication, eat dinner, sit around, medication, go to bed.

After nearly two weeks, a doctor finally showed up on the ward. He walked through the day room toward the nurses' station very quickly, looking down at his clipboard. Many of the patients grabbed his sleeve and started to ask him questions. It was obvious he didn't want to talk. He wanted to make it to the station as quickly as possible and close the day room door behind him. *Everyone's acting frantic,* I thought. *I'll approach him quietly and calmly and ask him to adjust my medication.*

After checking some records, he came out of the station and across the floor again. The arms reached out to him as though he were some sort of savior. I approached him from the front. "Doctor, my name is Pat—". He brushed me aside with the others. "Doctor?" But he kept walking quickly, much faster than before. "Please, I want to talk with you." The nurse was in front of him and opened the door with her key. He wasn't listening. I reached out and pushed my way in front of the other women. *Oh, my God,* I thought. *I'm acting just like everyone else, but he won't listen.* I grabbed the doctor's arm as he went out the door. The nurse grabbed my wrist tightly and pulled me away from him. I started breathing heavily, hyperventilating.

"You'll have to get control of yourself, young lady," the nurse warned me.

"I'm trying, I'm trying," I said through the short gasps of breath. The pains in my throat and chest from breathing heavily seemed too much to bear.

"If you're going to keep acting like that," the nurse said, "we'll have to put you in one of those little rooms to calm you down. Now you don't want that, do you?"

I definitely did not want that. I tried to keep the breathing under control.

The next week I saw a psychiatrist for ten minutes. He wanted the real names of my parents, so I gave them to him. I tried to explain so much to him in that short period of time. I was told my parents would be contacted and that if they agreed to sign me out I would be free to leave.

Another week went by. I got to see the doctor for another ten minutes. "Did you contact my mother?" I asked.

"Yes, she has been notified that you're here."

"Well, what did she say?"

"Your mother doesn't want to sign you out at this time. She would be responsible for you, and she doesn't feel that she can handle that kind of responsibility now. She requests that you be kept here under observation for a certain period of time."

"What kind of time? What do you mean?"

"Every three months a review board meets. That board consists of several doctors. After they meet, they will determine what will happen with you."

"Three months! Suppose after three months you determine that I am able to leave. Will I still need my mother's signature?"

"Yes."

"Well, what if she doesn't want to sign me out? Then what?"

"I don't know the answer to that. It might be up to the courts. Someone must agree to be responsible for you. Do you know of anyone who would agree to sign for you—someone that your mother would approve of?"

"That's a joke. Boy, this really puts her in the driver's seat, doesn't it?"

He shrugged his shoulders and slapped his hands down on his desk. "Well," he said as he stood up, "I'll be talking to you next week."

Shortly after that session, I was given extra ward privileges, such as freedom to attend church and watch television after it was time for everyone else to go to bed. I found out that the doctor had recommended that the privileges be granted. At our next meeting I thanked him.

"That's OK. I just wish I could do a little more for you. You still won't go before the review board for another sixty days. As long as you're going to be around for a time, maybe we should try talking about some of the difficulties that brought you here."

"Some of my difficulties? Why don't you start with my mother?" I said sarcastically.

"Why don't we discuss that at our next meeting?"

"What's the use, anyway? Talking about her isn't going to change the fact that she hasn't come to visit, or that she farmed me out to everyone else's home when I was a kid, or that she didn't care enough to look for me when I left home, or even here—you won't move unless she gives the word. She's even running you. So what good will it do to talk about her?"

"Do you feel bitter about her?"

"No, I don't feel bitter. I feel angry. I knew she loved me when I was in those other homes, at least I thought I did. I don't know what made her change. I know drinking can make you change. I'm angry because I don't understand. I can't put any of the pieces together. She went from one personality to another. She actually became different people, with different names and all. Can you believe that? She used to say that they were characters in her other lives. Can you believe that?"

"Listen, I have someone waiting outside. I think it would be good for us to pick up from here the next time I see you. If other things come to your mind you think are important, write them down."

The doctor and I had more, fairly profitable sessions. I was able to vent some of my feelings about my mother, and just to be able to do that was therapeutic. I still don't know for certain, but I think the doctor understood me, at least partially. At least he seemed willing to listen.

One afternoon I was informed I had a visitor waiting for me. I was led into a room where four or five families were sitting around tables, talking with one another. I saw my mother sitting at a table at the far end of the room. I felt a mixture of things—fear, excitement, gratitude, and mistrust. I walked slowly toward her, searching the expression on her face, wondering what kind of mood she was in, what personality she had taken on.

She smiled through tightly closed lips. I knew it was a fake. She remained seated as I reached the table. I bent over to kiss her and give her a hug. "How are you, Mom? I'm really glad to see you. It's been a long time. I thought you'd never come."

"Did you? Well, I do have three other children at home that need my attention. You don't want the same thing that happened to you to happen to them, do you?"

"No, no I don't. How are Susan and the other kids? How are they?"

"All fine." Her answer was stiff. Her eyes stared me down. They didn't blink at all. I looked down at the table to avoid her gaze.

"Mom, I'm sorry for all the trouble I've caused you. I know you have always done your best. I guess you've been through a lot that I've never been able to understand. But I am beginning to understand. I love you, I want you to know that." I was sincere in all my words. I really meant them. I reached out, put my hands over hers, and started to cry. Her hands were cold and didn't move, didn't even respond with a small twitch. "Mom, do you hear me? Mom, please say something—don't you understand?"

"Understand, understand—you don't understand the half of it!", she shot back. "After all I've sacrificed for you, you turn around and have given me nothing but misery. But you're the one who's in here, not me. You're the one that needs help. You're the one that needs the understanding, kiddo."

"Yes, you're right. I need help. I'm just learning to appreciate everything you did for me. You've given me a lot of good advice and taught me how to make decisions. Can you ever forgive me?"

"I'm glad you finally recognize the problems you have." Her stiffened body began to slouch in the chair and relax a bit.

"How is everyone?" I asked.

"They're all doing well." She reached into her pocket book. "Here, I brought you some things." She took out two cartons of cigarettes and some crayon drawings signed by my brothers and sister.

"It was real nice of you to bring me these things." I turned to see if the nurses were looking. "I don't want the nurse to see me crying," I whispered. "Listen, do you think that you can sign the papers to give me permission to be on the open ward? I'd be able—"

"I didn't come to talk to you about this," she said, cutting in and standing up as if to go. "If you insist on this kind of conversation, I'll have to leave."

"No, please don't go." She stared down at the hand that gripped her arm. "Please don't go. I won't talk about it anymore, I promise." I tried to gain control of my emotions as my mother sat down again.

"That's better," she said. "It's obvious from your condition that you should not be in an open ward. Who knows what you might do? I can't take on that kind of responsibility. I will not sign any papers. I want you to understand that you will be in here as long as I feel it is necessary. The quicker you straighten out, the quicker you'll be out. I have to go now." She touched my hand lightly and rose from her seat. "I won't be able to see you for quite a while," she said. "It's a long ride out here, and I do work, you know."

"I know. Will you write? I'll write to you if you want."

"That's fine with me. Just don't try to sneak any letters to the children. Is that clear?"

"Yes, that's clear." I put my arms around her and kissed her on the cheek. Then she turned and walked away. When I knew she wouldn't turn around, I picked up my cigarettes and pictures and let an aide lead me back to the day room.

14

When Can I See My Baby?

Drugs and alcohol flowed freely throughout the women's ward. Painters, electricians, and other workers from the outside brought them. Often they took money in exchange, but more often they were interested in getting sexual favors. I was assigned to the kitchen after a while, and there was absolutely no hospital supervision. During the mornings, the patients who had gone through electroshock therapy were wheeled into the kitchen after they had filled up all the recovery-room space. The patients were tied to their stretchers with rubber cord and had rubber sticks jammed into their mouths to keep them from swallowing their tongues. They had looked better before they went in for their "therapy." I kept my mouth shut and my emotions under control after getting my first look at the aftermath of electroshock. I lived in fear that it would be used as punishment if I acted up.

I had been going through so much turmoil that I didn't even notice I'd missed two menstrual periods. When I finally became aware of it, I reported to the nurse. She said it might be due to the heavy dose of Thorazine I was taking. A few days later I was sent down to one of the medical doctors for an exam. After it was over, he told me I was about three months pregnant.

When I got over the initial shock, the questions piled up. Who was the father? How did this happen? *I can't let my baby live in this place,* I thought. *What will they do with it?* I was due to see the psychiatrist soon. Maybe he would help me.

As usual, I sat in the chair opposite the doctor. But this time I didn't speak, I just stared at the floor. "I heard about the pregnancy," he said.

"I'm sure you did."

"I want you to know that we are going to try to help you."

I looked up at him for the first time. Was he telling me there was a chance I could leave this place?

"We are trying to arrange for you to go to a home for unwed mothers in New York City that may have space available shortly. It's not for sure, but we are trying to work it out."

"And my mother, does she know?"

"Yes, she knows."

"Not about being pregnant—does she know about the home? Will she allow it?"

"We are still talking to her. I don't think it will be necessary to go to the courts. I don't think she wants that."

"What happens after the baby is born? Will I be forced to come back here?"

"What happens to the baby is up to you. You are the natural mother. You might decide to keep it or else give it up for adoption to people who will be able to take good care of it. You must think of what is best for the child. In the meanwhile, we've asked your mother to try to get some adequate clothing for you. You know, sturdy shoes and some maternity dresses. We explained to her that it was possible to obtain some of these things from the Salvation Army, or perhaps her local church. In the meanwhile, we will cut down the amount of Thorazine you'll be taking and give you vitamins. It looks like you'll be leaving soon. And in case I don't see you again, I want you to know that I think you're a good kid. I also don't think that you belong in here. When you get out, keep yourself out of trouble. Discipline yourself. You know something else? I think it's a miracle that you have gone through as much as you have and have not been permanently scarred. You must have a bunch of guardian angels or something."

My mother was the one who had to drive me to the home for unwed mothers. We didn't speak much during the trip. I knew there was some kind of control she had over me, so I kept the conversation light, fearful that I might offend her in some way.

My room was on the top floor of the house. The house was run by women who had the best interests of the girls at heart. The house mother took my arm as I came through the front door and told me where my room was. "The climb up the stairs will be good exercise for you," she said. Her face was kind, her voice soft, and her smile sincere. After we were shown around, Mom handed the house mother my medicine given by the doctor and a shopping bag of clothes.

"When I come to visit, we'll go out and buy you some support shoes," Mom said. "You're not that big yet, so it can wait."

"I love you, Mom" I said as I hugged her.

"I love you, too. But I have to go now. So long, sweetie. Please take care of yourself. I'll be seeing you soon." She seemed so gentle. How could she turn herself on and off like that? She was becoming more and more of a mystery to me.

Most of the girls in the home were bitter but quiet, and

some tried to be tough. All of us pretty much kept to ourselves, except for the evenings, when we would gather down in the main living room to watch television.

On a hot night in July the labor pains began. The house mother timed the contractions, and at around five o'clock the next morning she decided it was time for me to go to the hospital.

"It's better for you to go now, before the other girls wake up," she said. "It's easier on everyone that way. Also, you won't be coming back here when you have the baby."

"Where will I be going?"

"You will be going to St. Zita's. That's over on 14th Street. It's sort of like a convent, but more like a halfway house for women who have no place to go. Pat, I think you should give the baby up for adoption. We've spoken to you about this before. Someone who can't have children as you can will give your child a good home. You can't do that yourself, and you must think of the baby. Won't you please do it?"

"I don't know. I just don't know." The contractions began again.

"Let's get you to the hospital." We walked down the stairs, out the front door, and then the few blocks to the hospital. She kept timing my contractions the whole way. Once she had admitted me and had me put in a wheelchair, she touched my shoulder softly and said, "I wish you the best. I have to go now. I must be back before the other girls wake up."

The nurse wheeled me into the elevator, and we went up. She helped me undress and placed a wrinkled white hospital gown on me. The contractions got stronger and closer together. I began to scream and cry, but the nurse

walked out. As the pain intensified, I kept calling out for my mother.
The nurse came back into the room. "Where is your husband, honey? Is he on the way?"
"I'm not married," I said. I turned my head and tried to conceal the tears.
"You'll be OK, honey." She took my hand and held it tightly. I didn't want to let it go. "I'll be back in a minute. Just hold on," she said, and then walked out again.
I screamed for her to come back. The pain got worse and worse.

"It's a boy," the doctor said. The maternity ward was lined with beds. I lay between two other young mothers. When feeding time came, I waited for my baby to be brought to me so that I might nurse him. The nurses walked in and handed the other mothers their babies. My baby was not given to me.
"Where is my baby?" I asked one nurse.
"I don't know. You'll have to speak to the doctor."
I waited in bed. No one came the entire day. At each feeding I was informed that the doctor would be down to speak with me. I was worried and confused. Was my baby dead? Was he sick? Had they signed my name and given him over for adoption? What happened?
The next morning, three doctors came to my bedside. "I have something to tell you about your baby," one of them said. "I'm sorry that you had to wait so long, but there were certain tests that had to be done."
"Yes—yes. What's wrong?"
"Your baby," the doctor continued, "is mongoloid."
"Mongoloid, what does that mean?"
"Well, aside from the fact that he is mentally deficient, he is also extremely physically deformed."
"I don't understand. What are you talking about?"

"The child, if he lives, will grow up retarded. He looks physically abnormal. His ears are very pointy, his tongue is long, his eyes are slanted, and he has webs of skin between his fingers. We have no idea how long he will live, because he has a congenital heart disease."

"When can I see my baby?" I asked the doctor.

"The nurse will take you to see him. We have him isolated in a special room"

"Why? Are you afraid he might frighten someone?" I said angrily.

"No, of course not. We have him separated for his own good. When you see him, I don't want you to be frightened. We have him in a special oxygen tent. We're watching him very closely.

"I'm sorry. I didn't mean to sound off at you. Everything just seems to be so mixed up." The doctor nodded his head wearily, and the three of them left the room.

I had named my little boy David, after King David in the Scriptures. He was going to be brave and strong, just like his namesake.

The first few times I saw David, I was not allowed to hold him. He couldn't be moved from his tent, so I talked to him through the glass partition that separated us. "Don't worry, David. I know how you look. Most people wouldn't want to keep their child if he looked like you do. But don't you worry. I'm going to find a job and an apartment and take you home and love you. I will never ever give you away."

I left the hospital, eventually, and was taken to St. Zita's. The nuns who ran the home were a lot nicer than the occupants. Most of the women were older than I was, and none of them were particularly friendly. I suppose I seemed the same to them. I was secretive and rarely spoke to anyone unless they inquired of me first. Most of my days were spent in the chapel, praying or watching the nuns pray. I wanted them to talk to me, but they seemed too absorbed in what they were doing. I wanted them to help me put some things back together, wanted them to tell me about the God they were praying to. But the scenario was always the same: The nuns would walk in, kneel at the altar, and pray for about fifteen minutes. Then they would file out silently, clutching their rosaries. I often looked right at them, but nobody smiled. Outside of the chapel they smiled and laughed, but they didn't talk to me about their God. Couldn't they see how desperate I was? I hoped that silently I could alert them to how much I needed God. I wanted to plead to Him, to ask Him what had gone wrong.

As soon as I was allowed to leave St. Zitas, I began looking for work. I found a waitress job on 77th Street and rented a room at a women's residence hall on 88th Street. I would visit the hospital when I was able, and I was now allowed to hold David for short periods of time. I tried to imagine what things would be like for David when he was ten years old, but I never let the thoughts get too far. I had to steel myself, had to fight off the tears, couldn't let emotions get in my way. I had to get off the merry-go-round I was on.

One evening, shortly after getting home from work, I received a call from a nurse at the hospital. "Would you mind coming down?" she said.

"What happened? Is the baby OK?"

"Your baby has taken a turn for the worse. Would you please come down?"

A doctor at the emergency room desk grabbed my elbow and led me to a couch in a waiting area. He was young and nervous. A nurse joined him and then came over to sit next to me. "Your baby," the doctor began, "has taken a turn for the worse."

"What does that mean?" I asked him. "Does it mean he's dead?" I braced myself, even though I knew what the answer would be.

"I'm afraid so. I know this is difficult for you, but we would like to do an autopsy on him."

"Does that mean you're going to cut him up and pull out his insides? I won't let you do that to my baby. No!"

"I know how this makes you feel," the doctor went on. "But if we can do an autopsy, we may be able to find out what caused his death and then be able to help other children. Can you understand that?" He was talking very gently now.

"Yes, if that's the reason, then I guess—yes."

The nurse handed me some papers and showed me where to sign. After I signed, I asked the doctor if I could see my baby. He led me into a room with cabinets built right into the wall. He walked over and spoke softly to another man. The doctor came back and told me once again how sorry he was. He touched my shoulder and left.

The other man led me to one of the cabinets and pulled out the drawer. It was too big to hold David; he looked like a little doll by comparison. His eyes were closed, and his tiny hands had been crossed one over the other, a thin string tying them together. I reached out and touched his forehead. It was cold. But then, the whole room was cold.

I don't know how long I stood there. "I think it would be better if you left now," the man finally said. "Would you like us to call someone for you? Do you have any family or friends?"

"No, that's OK. I'll be all right."

I don't remember the subway ride home. I wasn't

feeling anymore, wasn't crying. As soon as I walked into my small room, I began screaming at God. "I hate you. Are you satisfied. I can't even cry anymore. I hate you, I hate you, I hate you!" I undressed mechanically, turned off the light, and got into bed. After covering myself with blankets, I tried to rock myself to sleep. I was numb, in shock. I stayed in the same position all night and didn't sleep. When morning came, it took every ounce of strength I had to get out of bed.

The shrill sound of the phone filled the room.
"This is St. Vincent's Hospital calling. We'd like to know what arrangements you've made for your baby's burial."
"Arrangements?"
"Yes, for burying your baby."
"No, I haven't made any arrangements. What should I do?"
Do you have a church or minister?"
"No, but there is a church in Floral Park, where I used to live, a Methodist church."
"Give me the name of the church, and I'll make the arrangements for you."
I went to my window and opened it wide. The breeze was refreshing. "Maybe I'll take the day off," I thought out loud. "Maybe I'll go to the park, take a walk, lie in the grass. Yeah, maybe I'll just do that.

Ah, what's the use? I'd only have to come back to this crummy place anyway. What's wrong with me? Why does God do these kinds of things to people?"
"You're not my God," I screamed angrily. "You don't care at all what happens to me." I couldn't cry. All I could do was moan. The tears wouldn't come. There was no relief. The heaviness remained.

I wanted to deny God, but somewhere in the depths of my being I knew Him. But where? What was separating us? I cried out again, "Why God, why, why, why. . . . "

A knock came at the door. "Are you all right in there?" someone said.

"Yes, yes." I swallowed heavily. "I'm fine." I tried to make my voice sound normal. Still sitting on the balls of my feet in the middle of the floor, I had my arms crossed in front of me. I fell down in that position, staring at my knees. The tears wouldn't come.

I knew I had to shake it off and go to work. Working was important to me. My shift was from ten in the morning till ten at night. I needed the money and the therapy the long hours offered me. I was able to smile throughout that day, even though my emotions were in pieces. I had to be strong.

Early the next morning, the minister from the Methodist church in Floral Park called. "I have made arrangements to bury your child," he said. "Plan to be here at the church at ten tomorrow morning, and we'll drive to the cemetery."

"How is the body going to be brought there?"

"Arrangements have already been made to get the body here. All you have to do is get yourself here."

As soon as he hung up, I called my mother.

"Mom, this is Pat. I don't know how to tell you this, but the baby died. I'm coming out to Floral Park tomorrow to meet the minister and bury the baby." I waited, hoping for an invitation to come to the house.

"It's probably good for everyone that the child died," she said. "I don't know why you had to involve the minister in this town. We have to live here, too, you know."

"Yes, but I didn't know what else to do. Anyway, do you think that after the funeral I could stop at the house for a visit?"

"That is out of the question. I don't want you anywhere near this house or the kids. If you come here, I'll call the police. Is that clear?"

"But why?"

"Do you think you're the right kind of influence on the children?"

"Well, they don't have to know anything. I won't tell them, I promise."

"No. I don't want you here under any circumstances."

"Fine," I said angrily. "If that's how you feel, then it's fine with me." I slammed the receiver down and cursed loudly. "I don't need you," I said. "I don't need anyone!"

The next morning I took the train to Floral Park and walked to the church. Along the way I watched all around me in the hope that I would get a glimpse of one of my brothers or my sister. My heart ached to see them.

I arrived at the church and asked for the minister. His secretary introduced us, and we immediately left for the cemetery. We didn't speak the entire time. I was embarrassed and ashamed to look at him, because I knew that he must have been aware of all the details.

When we arrived at the cemetery, we were led by an attendant to a small plot in the farthest corner of the lot. Right next to the hole was a small plywood box.

"Is the baby in there?" I asked.

"Yes, he is," the minister said.

"But the box. I thought that—"

"Don't worry about the box," he interrupted. "It's strong."

"Where's the stone?"

"There is none. It's not necessary."

"Why? Is it because he was illegitimate?" I looked around the grounds. There were only a few stones; the other plots were unmarked. "What kind of cemetery is this: Is this a potter's field?"

"Please."

"Open the box. I want to see my baby. Maybe he's not there."

He put his arm around my shoulder. "He is there, but don't have the box opened. I understand that they did an autopsy on him, and it would be much better if the box were left closed. Why don't we pray now." The minister said a few nondescript words as an attendant lowered the casket into the ground. The minister and I walked back to the car without speaking.

"I'll drive you back to the station," he said. The drive seemed long. I stared out the window the entire time. I was hoping he could say something encouraging, give me some profound spiritual message. But he never said a word the entire trip, just looked at the road. When we got to the train station, he opened the car door for me.

"Have a safe ride back," he said. *He probably doesn't know the answers either,* I thought.

"Thank you very much."

"Oh, that's OK," he responded. He waved at me a couple of times and then drove off.

"No, he doesn't know," I muttered to myself as I walked to the train platform. "He doesn't know at all."

15

Are You Sure You Want to Marry Me?

Sometimes in the morning, before I went to work, I would stop off at a church; it didn't matter which one. I just needed some comfort. I thought that God, if He lived anywhere, would live in a church building. In a Catholic church I would light candles. In a Protestant church I would sit in a pew and pray.

Something drew me to pray. Maybe it was just the comfort I received from being able to find some release for all my pent-up thoughts and emotions. Yet I didn't really believe there was any power in prayer. I usually came out of the churches feeling the same way I had when I went in. At times the release would be good, and I left with a sigh of relief.

My prayers were usually the same: "Help me get my life straightened out," or "I'm being good, Lord, so why don't You answer me. Why do I feel so alone, like You've taken a vacation," and always "Please help me, please help me."

One evening I began thumbing through an old Bible I hadn't looked at in several years. I found special comfort in the Psalms, especially the psalms of David. David was continually opening his heart to God. He was not afraid to tell God what was on his mind, was not afraid to lament. He was not afraid to reveal his innermost feelings and doubts. The psalm that spoke to me most powerfully was Psalm 88, especially the first four verses:

> Oh Lord God of my salvation, I have cried day and night before thee:
>
> Let my prayer come before thee: Incline thine ear unto my cry;
>
> For my soul is full of troubles: and my life draweth nigh unto the grave.
>
> I am counted with them that go down into the pit: I am as a man that hath no strength.

I understood my condition and knew that I needed God, but I was unable to make the connection. I knew He heard my plea, but I also knew something was blocking the cementing of the relationship. And I didn't know what that something was.

I needed some stability in my life. I needed some familiar people around me, people who could lift me up when I needed it. I gave Leo a call to see if he would take me back and let me work. I was fearful of what he would say but my fears were unfounded. He and Phyllis welcomed me back with open arms.

Leo let me live in a furnished room in the basement of the luncheonette. With my room and meals taken care of, I could save some money again. Work and save and stay healthy—those were my immediate goals. I still had a tremendous desire to make something of myself. But I felt very much out of things because I didn't have a high-school diploma, that piece of paper that would open up a lot of job possibilities for me.

After working and saving for a little over a year, I signed up for evening classes at a local high school. My class had nearly a hundred students in it. Most of us sat on the floor or on the radiators. I was excited and diligent for a few weeks, but then I got bored and quit. I blamed it on the crowded conditions, the long trip from work to the city, the snow, the cold—anything I could think of. It seemed as though I had discipline in every area except the one in which I most desired to achieve it. I needed basic skills to achieve, but I lacked the discipline to develop them. I just kept setting myself up for failure.

I would often search the papers, looking for a job that would propel me in the direction I wanted to go—up. Sometimes when I answered the ads and was told I didn't have enough experience, I would volunteer to work for free, just to get the experience.

One day I answered an ad for an opening at a real estate office. The office was small, unadorned, with only four desks and a few pictures on the walls. The woman who owned the office, Lee, agreed to train me and teach me how to keep the books and manage apartment buildings, and she gave me hints on renting and selling. It was agreed that I would work for thirty dollars a week plus commission.

I was elated. It was just the chance I was looking for. I was to start the following week. That week's wait gave me a chance to give my notice to Leo and go look for a night job at another restaurant. There was no way I could make it on thirty dollars a week, and the commissions would not be coming until I learned the business fairly well.

I found another job at a restaurant only three blocks

from the real estate office. I bought some nice outfits to wear at the office, but I had to make a good impression on everyone. I was not going to let this chance slip by.

Lee was patient with me and would encourage me even when I made silly or simple mistakes. She knew I was anxious to learn and get ahead. It was a long time, nearly a year, before I made my first commission. It was a small one, but it made me feel good about myself.

I began taking real estate classes so I could get my broker's license. The business was expanding, and Lee was going to need more help soon to keep up with all the work.

One morning Lee announced that she was going out to Nevada to file for a divorce, and that she would be leaving the office in my care. During her absence, she called from time to time. Each time we spoke she planned to extend her visit there.

One afternoon I received a very surprising call from her. "Pat, this is Lee. How's everything going?"

"Fine, just fine. Are you still in Nevada?"

"Yes. Listen, I'll get right to the point. I'm planning to stay out West and invest some money. I'm going to sell the business and was wondering if you'd like to buy it. I thought I'd give you first crack at it. Did you hear me?"

"I'm sorry. I was just a little shocked. I was just wondering how I'd be able to get the money. Also, since I don't have a broker's license, how could I buy the business? It wouldn't be legal."

"One way we could work it would be for me to sell you 49 percent of the business and let you use my name and license till you get your own. Then you can buy the rest. How does that sound to you?"

"It sounds fine, but how much money do you want?"

"For 49 percent, I'd say around twenty-six hundred."

"Give me some time to think about it, OK? I don't know where I'm going to come up with that kind of money. I'll call you back in about a week?"

"That's fine, I'll talk to you then."

Where would I get money like that, I thought. *A bank? I don't have any credit with a bank. Leo? Leo doesn't have it, either. If he did he wouldn't have to work at that extra catering job.*

I did get the money, from a gentleman named Mr. Maguire. While I was living in my first apartment in New York City, that place I was kicked out of after getting back from the hospital, I hired myself out briefly to an "escort" service as some of my friends had suggested. Mr. Maguire was one of the people I went out with fairly steadily. He took me to dinner and the theater and paid me a lot of money to be seen with him. He was very kind to me, not forceful at all. All my associations in that business made me nervous, though, and I didn't last too long.

I didn't know if Mr. Maguire was still around, but I checked through the phone book till I found a Maguire with a first name that looked familiar. I had to make several calls until I found the right man. It took Mr. Maguire a few minutes to remember who I was, but he had no trouble once I refereshed his memory a bit.

Evidently, he thought I was sincere in my request for the loan, because he granted it without any hesitation. The only suggestion he made was that I call Lee and get her to lower the price for the whole operation. He looked at the profit and loss statement and told me the business was not worth as much as Lee was asking. Lee was a little reluctant to go down on her original price, but she was also glad to be able to sell the whole business at once.

I worked hard, made some mistakes over the next

couple years, and had some small successes. I was twenty-three years old and felt that for the first time my life was going in the right direction. I moved into a brand new "prestige" apartment with another girl; *All part of the dream,* I thought.

But the desire for that "piece of paper" still haunted me. People often asked what school I had graduated from. I wanted to be able to rattle off the name of some highbrow Eastern college the way many of my business acquaintances could.

Late in the summer of 1966, I saw an ad in the paper from another management firm looking for help. Though the ad indicated that help was wanted in the office, I thought it might be an opportunity to bring several accounts into my office. I called and made an appointment to see a Mr. Frank Fernandez.

The next morning, I showed up on time but then had to wait for an hour while his secretary tried to locate him. I was extremely annoyed. "May I please have a piece of paper and an envelope? I would like to leave Mr. Fernandez a note. I can't wait any longer," I finally said. I scrawled the note quickly and handed it back to the secretary. "Kindly hand this to Mr. Fernandez when he returns."

I had lost my morning and there was a lot of work to do. Around one o'clock, Mr. Fernandez returned my call. A deep, resonant voice at the other end of the line said, "I'm really sorry for making you wait. I got held up at a breakfast meeting. I read your note and would like to make another appointment to see you."

"How about tomorrow at the same time?" I asked.

"I promise I'll be here. You won't have to wait for even a minute."

The next morning I arrived right on time. Mr.

Fernandez walked out of his office to greet me and escort me in. He motioned me over to a large leather chair in front of his desk. He sat in his own large swivel chair and leaned back. His broad shoulders reached to both sides of the wide chair. He had just a touch of silver in his otherwise jet-black hair. It was the first time I had ever looked at a man and felt an immediate attraction. I estimated him to be in his fifties.

He eyed me carefully as he peered over the top of his Ben Franklin glasses. He smiled and said, "That's the first time anyone has ever written me a note like that. I'm usually the one who writes the notes. But," he continued, "I want you to know I admire you for it. You were correct. It's very unusual, though, for a job applicant to write such a note." He took the glasses off and twirled them. He smiled at me again, as though he were trying to figure me out.

I couldn't speak. I was captivated. Realizing I might have been staring, I blushed and began looking around his office. There were photographs on one of the shelves. "Who are they?" I asked, pointing to the picture of a young man and young lady about my age.

"They're my children."

"Oh." I came back to my senses quickly. I was talking to a married man. Losing my senses just as quickly, I asked, "Why don't you have a picture of their mother?"

"Their mother? Oh, she died some time ago."

"That's too bad. Mr. Fernandez," I went on, "let me explain to you why I'm here."

"I know why you're here. You came about the management job."

"Yes, but I'd like to explain—"

"Where do you live?"

"On 47th Street, at the Embassy House."

"That's a nice location."

"Mr. Fernandez, I have my own real estate office on East 49th Street. I believe you have a building there, right down the block from my office."

"How do you know that?"

"I saw your name and address in the owners' book. I manage two buildings on that street," I said. He continued to smile. I put my elbow on the arm of my chair. I lowered my head into my hand and started blushing again. "Mr. Fernandez, please, you're making this very difficult." I raised my head, and we both began to laugh. "Mr. Fernandez, I'm trying to discuss business with you."

He rose from his chair. "Can we talk over lunch? Do you have time? Please join me," he said.

I felt uneasy looking up at him from my seat. "Well—I guess so."

"Fine. Then let's get out of here." He grabbed me by the elbow and ushered me out of his office and down the stairs. I was speechless.

He smiled the whole two blocks to the restaurant. "I don't know what to say to you," he said. "You have taken me completely by surprise."

I watched my feet as I walked. I looked up and around in every direction I could think of, but not at him. "I'm trying to figure you out, too," I said.

At the restaurant, he ordered lunch for both of us. "Pat, may I call you Pat? If I have taken you by surprise, you have taken me by surprise as well. There's something about you that's different. You know, I'm from the old school. I believe people should be on time for appointments, and I'm sorry about yesterday. I believe that you should go after business, and I see you feel exactly the same way."

"How do you know? You never gave me a chance to finish my conversation."

"I didn't want to finish because I was afraid you would leave. You see, I don't let any of my properties out for management. I keep them all in my office. I was afraid that once I told you that, our meeting would be over. I had to think quickly to keep you from going."

"This is like a movie," I said. "I don't know what to say. But I know what you're talking about. There's something about you that's different, too."

"How old are you?" he asked.

"I'm twenty-eight," I lied. "How old are you?"

"Uh—fifty-three, but you look younger than twenty-eight."

"No—I'm twenty-eight."

We had lunch together every day. We had dinner together every evening for the next two weeks. Sometimes he would call and ask me to go out to breakfast. The day after we met, he sent a dozen roses over to my office. I was showered with attention. We would often go dancing after dinner, sometimes staying out till four in the morning. We would walk around my block again and again, just talking.

I felt uneasy about lying to him about my age. One evening he came over to my apartment just before dinner. He found me sitting on the sofa, crying. I knew that if he found out I had lied to him, he wouldn't want me back.

"Why are you crying?" he asked, holding my face gently in his large hands.

"I lied to you," I said.

"Lied? About what?"

"About my age—I'm not twenty-eight. I'm only twenty-three."

He leaned forward and kissed my tears. "Hey, don't worry about that. You don't have to be embarrassed about that or what you've done, or anything. You're very special to me."

I started to sob louder. "You wouldn't say that if you knew what I was really like, some of the things I've done. You don't know anything about me or my past."

"But I want you to tell me about it, though. I really don't think there's much you could say that would surprise me. Besides, I want to know all about the woman who will be the mother of my children."

"What? What are you talking about?" I looked up at him. The thumb of his right hand wiped my tears away.

"I want you to be the mother of my children. Will you marry a dirty old man like me?"

I started laughing and crying at the same time. "You're not a dirty old man. Besides, I'm not sure you'd want anything to do with me if you knew my background."

"Don't worry. You're a diamond in the rough. You'll become the brightest jewel on my diadem. I know enough. Will you marry me?"

"Only if you'll let me talk to you about my past and tell you everything first."

"Fine, start talking. I've got all evening."

I told him all about my background, all the experiences I'd been through, every detail. He didn't say anything, just held my hand tightly the entire time. When I finished, he didn't react at all. He got up and walked toward the door. "Pat, I want you to have lunch with me tomorrow."

"Sure. Same place as always?"

"Right." He kissed me on the forehead and left. I

threw myself down on the couch and cried. "Why did you tell him, you dummy? Why? Why?"

I woke up late the next morning. It was Saturday and I was accustomed to going to work. But I was too wrung out to even think about work. I knew I wouldn't function properly.

I barely had enough time to make it to lunch. I dressed quickly and walked the mile to the restaurant. I sat at the table we usually sat at. I waited fifteen minutes, half an hour, forty-five minutes. I thought strongly about leaving.

He finally ran in, all out of breath. "I'm glad you didn't leave," he said through the gasps. "I was afraid you'd be gone."

He sat down across from me and took hold of my hands. The waiter brought coffee for both of us and left the menus. I watched Frank closely. He kept his eyes on his coffee for nearly a minute before saying anything. When he finally did say something, he blurted it out. "You're very special, very special. I have something I want to give you." With one hand he started fumbling through his coat pockets. "Here, this is for you."

He handed me a small black box. I looked up at him. "What is it?"

"Open it and find out."

I opened the top slowly. Inside was a beautiful diamond ring. "I'm not too good at proposing," he said. "Maybe this should have been done in a more romantic setting."

"Are you sure you want to marry me?"

"Don't have such a negative opinion of yourself. I'm the one who will be getting the better deal. I'm a difficult man to live with."

"I can't believe that's true. Are you sure? Do you really want to marry me?"

"I know what I want, and I think you do, too. I can give you the security and guidance you've never had. You name it. Most important, though, you're the kind of woman I want."

"I love you, too. I can't believe this is really happening to me," I said through tears of joy.

He took the ring out of the box and put it on my finger. "It fits," I said. "How did you know my size?"

"I didn't. I just guessed. If you don't like the ring, we can exchange it."

"No, it's beautiful, just beautiful." We leaned across the table and kissed.

"Yesterday," he said, "you told me some things you thought would make a difference to me. Now I have some things to tell you. Please hear me out. Remember when you asked me about the pictures in my office?"

"Yes, your children."

"Well, I told you their mother was dead, and she is. What I didn't tell you is that I married again." I pulled my hands away from him. "Please let me finish. I married six years ago, and it hasn't worked out. We are in the final stages of getting a divorce. It had nothing to do with you. It's been coming for a long time. Meeting you, however, has encouraged me to speed up the proceedings."

"Why didn't you tell me this before?"

"Because I knew you wouldn't go out with me."

"You're right about that. How long will the proceedings take?"

"You ask that as though you don't trust me. But I can understand how you feel. I don't know exactly how long. We are trying to work out a settlement. She's asking for a great deal. I would hope that it won't take more than a few weeks."

"Have you two had any children?"

"No."

"Where are you living now?"

"I know this is going to sound strange. We are still living in the same house, but in separate rooms."

I pulled away. "You're right. That does sound strange. I don't want to be the cause of anyone's marriage breaking up. I don't want to be anyone's mistress, either. I've been working too hard to straighten my life out. I don't want to fall into any traps."

"Please believe me. First you have to understand something. There are two floors to my apartment. My wife and I sleep on different floors. Anyhow, my attorney has advised me to move out during the proceedings. So I thought I would take an apartment in the same building you're living in." I searched his face, suspicious of his intentions. "I know what you're thinking, Pat. Will you please trust me?"

"I don't know. I just don't want to—" I shook my head and then grabbed his hand. "Yes, yes, I'll trust you. But if you're trying to pull something on me, I'll—"

"You'll see. I'm not trying to pull something on you. You won't regret this, I promise. I just want to make you happy."

"I want to make you happy, too." We sat quietly for a few minutes, all smiles. "I'd like for you to meet my mother," I said. "I can't wait to tell her about us."

"Anything you like. I want to do whatever pleases you. By the way, do you mind if I put your name on the payroll? Then I can pay the rent for my new apartment out of that. I'd rather not have any records in my office of rents being paid to another management company. It's just for looks. You'll be listed as getting a salary, but that money will go for the rent. Also, I don't want anyone to know where I am until the divorce is final."

"That's fine with me. I just want to do whatever pleases you."

16

His Fair Lady

Frank never talked much about the divorce proceedings, saying only that it was going to be a very messy situation and that he wanted to keep me out of it. One evening, over dinner at my apartment, he finally began to talk about what was happening. His expression was strained; he'd been on a real emotional merry-go-round and wasn't doing too good a job of covering the effects. "Everything is signed," he said. "I'm going down to Mexico. She'll have an attorney representing her there."

"You look kind of depressed. Are you sure everything's OK?"

"Well, I agreed to give her more than I thought I should have."

"Why?"

"Because I didn't want to drag this thing out. It's not fair to you."

"How much did you give her?"

"Thirty-six thousand for each of the first two years and twenty thousand for each of the next nine years. She also gets to stay in the house for another four months."

"What? Where are you going to get that kind of money? I never heard of anything like that. Do you make that much?"

"Yes, sweetie, I make that much and a whole lot more. I think she would have been entitled to that much if there had been any children. But there aren't any."

"That's ridiculous. I'll wait. Don't do this on account of me. Fight it."

"I'm not agreeing just because of you. I signed because of what I want, too. I want to be with you. I don't want to wait any longer."

We flew down to Mexico and got married in a small Spanish court several hours after Frank straightened things out with the lawyer. I said "I do," but I couldn't understand what the judge was saying. Frank had to nudge me and give me my lines when it was time. It didn't seem like much of a ceremony. As soon as the service was over I made a request. "Frank, would you mind—I've always wanted to have a church wedding. Do you mind if we have the ceremony over again in a church?"

"Not at all. Let's fly to California, and you can pick out a church that you like."

We went to La Jolla, California, and I called a Methodist church and made the arrangements. I called my mother and arranged for her and Susan to come to the ceremony. I sent Mom the money for the plane fare, and also a little extra to buy nice dresses for the wedding.

The arrangements were all made. Everything went precisely as I had planned. Imagine my surprise, then, when my mother walked into the church wearing a house dress and bedroom slippers. I was stunned. Susan was wearing a nice dress. *Why couldn't Mom do something nice just this once?* I thought.

Frank saw her, too, and read my mind. He leaned over and whispered, "Don't let it upset you. This is our special day. You don't have to worry about anything anymore.

Don't worry about your mother. Put your head up and act as though you didn't notice."

"But why is she doing this?"

"I doesn't matter. What matters is you and me, right?"

"Right." We hugged. I ran over to my mother as she came in the door. "Oh, Mom, I'm so glad you came. Isn't this exciting?"

"Congratulations, honey," she said, and then she kissed my cheek.

It was a small wedding, but it was so beautiful. I had bought a beautiful lace mantilla to wear as a veil because it was Spanish and Frank was Spanish. I cried throughout the whole ceremony, and all during the reception I had tears in my eyes. My mom and Susan left quickly and didn't stay around for much of the reception. I did as Frank told me and pretended not to notice.

We spent our honeymoon in San Francisco. We walked through the parks, had dinner on Fisherman's Wharf, and strolled through Chinatown. It was the most romantic time I had ever known. But even with all that romance, Frank still remembered the business. One afternoon, as we were walking through a park close to our hotel, Frank said, "I want to visit a bakery while I'm here."

"Why?"

"So I can write off this trip. I own a bakery in New York."

"You do? My, you're full of surprises, aren't you?"

"I saved a few for you," he said with a smile.

The honeymoon was much too short, and before I knew it I was back in New York. Frank said that the first order of business when we got back was for me to meet his son, Peter.

He called Peter as soon as we returned and told him

that he had gotten married. I was a little puzzled about why Frank hadn't invited his son—hadn't even told him. But I didn't ask any questions.

The first meeting I had with Peter was awkward, especially since he was older than I was. But he made me feel comfortable and acted as though I had been a part of the family for years.

Frank wanted me to sell my business and work with him. I was able to do that without too much trouble.

The first day at Frank's office, he called his whole staff together and introduced me. Then he took me around and introduced me to each person individually, telling me what his function was. Peter stood off in the corner of the large office and smiled his approval.

"Let me show you the bakery now," Frank said. He took me downstairs, and we walked through the plant. The production area was more than a block long and about half a block wide. I was amazed.

"This is a wholesale bakery," Frank said. "You probably thought I ran a little corner store outfit, didn't you?"

"I didn't know what to think. I certainly didn't imagine this."

While we were at work, Frank got me familiar with the operation of the bakery and the management company. He wanted me to know all the ins and outs of each business. Even when we got back to the apartment each evening, my instruction went on. We didn't have all the disturbances of the office, so Frank could talk without being constantly interrupted.

Nearly four months to the day after we were married, we moved to the house Frank had had to vacate for his ex-wife. It was located on East 67th Street. "This house," Frank said, "is the old Bache Mansion." I had never seen anything so huge. Frank took a key and opened the double iron and glass doors.

The main floor was solid marble and was set off by a wide spiral staircase. "On the back right is an office I rent to a doctor. I also rent out the second and third floors, and the top two floors belong to us."

We walked through the main floor. Frank pressed the call button for an elevator. When we reached the top floor, he opened another door. Taking my hand, he led me through a series of ornately decorated rooms. After the tour, I sat down at the dining room table and cried. Frank had gone to the phone to make a call.

Frank's attorney, Byron Golden, who had come with us, asked "What's the matter, Pat?"

"It's all too much—all of this. I don't want to live here. I want to stay in our little apartment."

"You'll get used to it," Frank said, chuckling, from the other room.

"But it's not right. It's too much. It's too big."

"After a while, you won't even notice it," Byron said.

"I wanted to look for an apartment with Frank and choose furniture together and decorate it together. Everything is here, everything is done. You don't understand."

"I think I do," Byron said. "After you get used to the place, you can make the changes you want."

"You might not even want to make changes," I heard from the next room.

Our marriage was not the typical one in which couples grow and change together. Frank was set in his ways. I had to fit the mold he wanted to create for me, and I was delighted to do it. I relied very heavily upon his approval.

Frank loved me very much, and being loved was wonderful. I wanted very much to please him, and I learned that the best way to do that was to work hard at the business end of things, to produce more and more. I learned that the better I did at the office, the more affection I would receive at home. If there were days when he thought I didn't put forth much of an effort, affection was limited or withheld completely. Needless to say, this put a strain on the relationship.

During the first year of the marriage, Frank would take me shopping and choose my clothing. He bought me the kind of wardrobe that was pleasing to him. He showered me with gifts: diamonds, rubies, emeralds, and furs. We were constantly going to the theater, operas, and the ballet.

"You," he announced one evening, "are my fair lady. You were a diamond in the rough. Now look at you." He stood back proudly and admired me. At first I was pleased that I was pleasing him. In time, as I grew a bit wiser, I resented being called his "fair lady" because of what I thought it implied.

One afternoon, after my regular medical checkup, I was informed that I was pregnant. I ran all the way from the doctor's office to Frank's office (nine blocks). I bounded up the stairs and into Frank's office; I was breathless and unable to speak. One of the bakery salesmen sat across from him.

"Please," I gasped, "excuse us for one moment." Under normal circumstances, I never would have barged into his office like that, especially if there was a meeting going on. Frank was so surprised by my entrance that he was silent. The salesman quickly left the room. I closed the door behind him and leaned my body on the door for support.

"What is it?" Frank said. "It had better be important." He sat back in his chair. "Come on, tell me."

I waved a piece of paper in front of him. "This is it. This is it."

"What is it?" he asked.

"If you want to see it, come get it from me." I was trying to bait him into chasing me around the office. I walked around the floor, waving the paper. "Come and get it, come and get it," I teased. He came after me and pinned me against the window sill. I hid the paper behind my back. I taunted him some more. "You have to kiss me if you want to see it."

He kissed me and grabbed for the paper at the same time. "That," I said, "is from the doctor."

"I don't understand this at all," he said quizzically.

"What do you mean, you don't understand it? It says that I'm pregnant."

"Are you sure?"

"Am I sure? Just wait." I ran over to the phone and called the doctor. I told him to tell Frank. I stood there proudly and watched his eyes as the doctor gave the news to him. He hung up the phone and hugged me and swirled me around the room. Then, grabbing my hand, he whisked me down the stairs and across the street to a newsstand. He bought a whole box of cigars.

"I thought cigars were for after the baby was born," I said.

"Well, I'm going to give a few out before it happens. Let me call Peter and tell him the good news. He should be the first to know. Wait a second, I'll call him and ask him to go to lunch with us. Then I'll tell him."

At lunch he handed Peter a cigar and broke the news to him.

"Congratulations to both of you," Peter said. "You both must be very happy."

I felt as though I was the only one in the world who had ever gotten pregnant. I was so proud that I went right out and bought some maternity clothes. I couldn't wait until I filled them out. I thought I would be loved more by Frank because I was going to bear him a son.

Several weeks after the announcement, Frank left for his annual fishing trip up in northern Canada. He and some friends would fish and relax for an entire month. Just as he was about to leave, he said, "You take care of yourself and shim."

"Who's shim?"

"Shim" he announced, "is who you are carrying right now. We don't know whether it's going to be a she or a him, so we'll call it shim. I'll write to you when I can. Not much mail goes out from where I'm heading, though, unless a seaplane comes for it."

"That's fine. Don't worry about anything at the office. I'll take care of everything. Just have a good rest and a nice time."

Twelve days later I received my first letter from him:

My dearest,

It is 6:15 A.M. I am up and shaved and bathed. By 7 we shall be at Port Menier Rimouski. There we get off and take a four hour ride in a truck to the Potato River, where all the huge salmon await my skills. Tony, the doctor from Binghampton, is a nice fellow. As a matter of fact, the entire crew and all the passengers (male) are very nice.

I think a lot about the wonderful marriage you have given me and brag about you to Tony the doctor. I also think about the shape of things to come and about our shims and how nice it will be to have a lovely family with you. I know you must think about me sometimes. As I am away from you I become nicer to you and forget my nastiness. Don't work too hard, and please hold the railing when you go downstairs. Look both ways before crossing streets. I adore you and love you and shim very much.

Daddy

I loved receiving mail from him. He was right. When he went away on trips, I forgot his nastiness, and only the thoughts of all the good times would return. He had a way of charming me that could make me forget his meanness and how he acted toward me when I didn't live up to his expectations.

25 July

My dearest,

I am really missing you like crazy. I think of you much of the day, of shims and how lucky I am to have found you. I think of how good you are to me, and I am very proud of you. We certainly were meant for each other, and the Lord was good to have led us into each other's arms. We have something very precious and must keep it so always. I am looking forward to getting back to you, but, alas, no boats until Saturday. I love you and adore you my sweet, child bride.

Daddy

The routine was the same for each of these annual trips. While he was gone, I would try to do things that would make his return happy. I'd raise the rents in his commercial buildings and renovate the apartments in the residence dwellings—anything that would show an increase in the bottom line of the business ledger. The more I produced, the happier he was. The happier he was, the happier I was.

Throughout my pregnancy, I prayed that my baby would be born healthy. Those prayers were answered on January 17, 1968, when Eliot was born, a normal, healthy baby boy.

I was thrilled, and Frank was gloating and handing out cigars to everyone. I immediately started nursing the baby, spending all my time with him. I wanted so much to be the perfect mother and let my child know that I loved him very much.

A couple of weeks after Eliot was born, Frank wanted me to return to work. He said that the office was only a couple of blocks from the house and that I could go back to nurse the baby whenever I felt like it. "I want to stay home with Eliot," I protested.

"We'll get him a governess. It will make it easier for you. Besides, he sleeps all day. You can work part-time if you like." It was going to be a competition, I saw already, between my job, my husband, and my baby, to see who—or what—got the most attention.

17

What Happens When the Candy's Gone?

Frank had some impressive friends. Many of them were politicians or top executives in business. I learned to entertain them gracefully, either for personal dinner parties or political fund-raising occasions. There was no doubt that Frank had fashioned me into the kind of woman he wanted. I actually began to enjoy my new role.

One evening at dinner, Frank announced, "Pat, I have a surprise for you."

"What is it?"

"We have been invited by President and Mrs. Johnson to join them for dinner at the White House with the Shah of Iran."

"What?"

"That's right."

"The president?" He nodded as he sipped his coffee. "I didn't know you knew the president. You, are full of surprises. Speaking of surprises, I just found out that you've been lying to me."

"About what?" He sat up attentively in his chair.

"Well, I just saw your passport today. You've lied about your age. According to your passport, you were born in 1903. According to your pistol permit, you were born in

1905. And you say you're fifty-five. Now what's the truth?"

"So, you found me out. When we first met, I didn't want to tell you how old I was. I thought you might run away."

"So why did you wait so long?"

"Does it matter to you?"

"Of course not." I started to laugh.

"Hey, you changed the subject. Aren't you excited about going to the White House?"

"I guess so. I didn't vote for Johnson, you know."

"I'd rather you didn't tell anyone that."

"OK, I'll keep it to myself—and I'm glad we're going."

"You don't sound like it."

"I'm glad, I'm glad," I said, laughing. "I just think it's funny that you lied about your age, that's all."

It was June 11, 1968. Our rented black limousine pulled up in front of the White House. Frank took my hand as he led me through the front entrance. "You look like a million dollars," he said. I was wearing the Oscar de la Renta gown he had picked out for me. My hair was swept up off my shoulders, and I wore the emerald and diamond earrings he had given me for Valentine's Day. My long white gloves almost touched my elbows. He looked at me again and said, "I bet you're the youngest and most beautiful woman here." I felt like Cinderella being escorted by her Prince Charming through a make-believe castle. But something was missing.

"Are you nervous, Mrs. Fernandez?" Frank asked.

"Not at all, Mr. Fernandez." I smiled and nodded graciously. "This place looks like a fairy tale, though. How do they live with all these things? This place looks like a museum."

"They don't live with it. They entertain in these rooms."

"It all seems like such a waste." We joined the other guests, who stood around, sipping drinks. "This must be the room they dance in. Look how high the ceilings are. It looks like a ballroom."

After exchanging pleasantries with some of the other guests, it was time to join a reception line and be introduced to President and Mrs. Johnson. I tried to keep a straight face as the president winked at each woman.

Frank and I were seated at different tables, as were all husbands and wives. I studied the people closely. Most of them sat up stiffly and looked as though they had smiles starched to their faces. *I'll bet they're having more fun in the kitchen,* I thought.

The conversation at the table consisted mostly of empty chit-chat. There was no entertainment that evening because the country was still mourning the assassination of Senator Robert Kennedy.

Black men wearing white gloves and black and white formal service uniforms were serving our tables. *Wow,* I thought. *Martin Luther King just died and this scene looks as though it could be taking place on some Southern plantation.*

"Things haven't changed," I said out loud, shaking my head.

"What did you say?" the man next to me asked.

"Oh, nothing. I was just thinking out loud."

In his toast that evening, the Shah said, "You have never failed us so far, and I'm sure you would never fail us as you have never failed any people of any country."

After we had returned to our hotel room, I told Frank, "Most of the evening seemed cold. What was it all about?"

"Most of the people were invited because they made

big contributions to the party. They couldn't care less about each other."

"I don't know exactly," I said. "But I do know that no happiness comes from all this wealth and fame. I mean, doesn't it bother you that you're invited to places like the White House because of the amount of money you contribute? Wouldn't you rather be invited someplace because someone likes you, whether or not you have money? It's so unreal."

"Pat, it is real. It's part of life. Peoople respect you when they know you've earned your way. That's one of the qualities I respect most about you. You've been able to pull yourself up by your own bootstraps. You're not afraid of work. You pay your own way."

"But something's missing. I remember when I was a little girl. I didn't have any friends. But when I had a Hershey bar, the kids were all around me, and they each wanted a piece of it. When the candy was gone, so were they. Isn't this whole scene the same thing, like the kids and the Hershey bar?"

Judging from the look on my husband's face, I decided not to pursue the topic any further.

18

I Want You to Find Someone Else

I found out shortly after the White House experience that I was pregnant again. I was still nursing Eliot, and I had heard (apparently it was an old wives' tale) that it was impossible to get pregnant while you were nursing another child.

On January 8, 1969, our second child was born, a beautiful little girl named Cristina. Tensions between Frank and I mounted during our daughter's first year. It was the same old conflict. Frank wanted me to work, and I wanted to spend time with my children.

He was under a great deal of pressure at the time. He was trying to completely automate the bakery with equipment from Germany, equipment that would cost him close to a million dollars. I was getting jealous over the time he spent at work, trying to get the deal organized. All the aggravation Frank got at work he would bring home to me. Once the equipment arrived, he supervised the installation, which had to be exactly right. He wanted me to come down to the bakery more often to help take some of the pressure off him. There were times when he would scream and holler at me in front of the other employees. Other times, we would be walking home from work and he would explode into a sudden rage, yelling at me and hurling insults.

One afternoon, at the corner of Madison Avenue and 64th Street, his rage reached its limits.

"I am disgusted with everyone who works for me. I can't depend on my son to do anything, and now I can't depend on my wife to do anything," he screamed. People turned and stopped to watch his rage. I stood on the corner, taking it all in and choking back the tears.

"That's not true. You just don't appreciate what people do for you. No matter what Peter does, you don't appreciate it. You can't expect him to be like you. You two had different backgrounds."

"He certainly didn't have one like yours," he said with a snicker.

"No. But it's impossible to please you. No matter how much I work, it's never enough for you. You push yourself and everyone else much too far."

"What do you know?" he growled. "You came from the gutter."

For the first time, I hated him. I stared at him in disbelief. "Go back to the gutter where I found you," he yelled.

"You never found me in the gutter. Right now is the lowest I've ever been in my life." I turned on my heels, crying, and ran acrosss the street and down the block toward the house.

"Guttersnipe," he yelled.

I loved my husband very much, but the times of cruelty and verbal abuse continued. It was always connected with work.

Our third child, Eric, was born in July 1970. He brought us as much joy as had the other children. I wanted to spend as much time as I could with the children, but when I'd mention it, Frank would accuse me of not wanting to help him when he most needed it. His temper grew worse as the pressure grew. We often spent the weekends at a home Frank had bought in Bedford Hills, a quiet little village about an hour's drive north of the city. But even those periods were no longer a time of peace for him. Our marriage was suffering under the strain. One weekend I confronted him.

"I want you to find someone to take my place," I begged.

"Ready to desert in the line of fire, huh? Ready to run off when I need you."

"Frank, I've always been around when you needed me. But after you come back from your fishing trip next month, I want you to find someone else. I want to be with the kids, but when you come home from work I want the two of us to have a relationship. Our marriage is in trouble because of the business."

"You don't care about me or the business. You only care about yourself."

"That's not true. Let me remind you that when you married me you owned eighteen apartment buildings. You now own fifty. You never made me the legal owner of any of the properties or even put them under joint ownership. I own no stock in any of your corporations, and I've never asked you for anything. But if we don't look out for our marriage, we're not going to have one."

"What is that supposed to mean?"

"It means that we might become another divorce statistic."

"No one divorces me. I do the divorcing."

"I hope it doesn't come to that."

"Well, let me give you some food for thought. With your background, the children wouldn't be given to you. Have you thought of that? And don't forget that I have a lot of friends in the right places. I would see to it that you don't get the children."

His words frightened me. I had to find out if that was true. I called a close friend of his, a supreme court judge, and asked to see him. He agreed.

"Judge, I want to tell you all about my background." I proceeded to fill him in, even including some potentially damaging details. Then I asked, "Would a court take my children away from me?" Then I asked him if he would interfere in the case if Frank asked him to.

"Pat, you know better than that. I'm your friend and Frank's. I couldn't interfere."

"I believe that. I just want to be sure."

"Does Frank know you came to see me?"

"No, I know it would hurt him if he knew. His ego is really fragile."

"It would be better if you don't say anything."

The next month, when Frank went on his fishing trip, I covered the apartment buildings for new leases and increases in rents. When he returned, he found thirty-six thousand dollars worth of signed leases on his desk, with the rent increases spelled out right in the contracts. He was pleased, and it eased some of the tension. I continued to work and slowly became more involved with the bakery, which I intensely disliked.

"Once the bakery starts to pay for itself, things will be all right," he said. I felt sincerely that our relationship was on the mend.

19

A Turn for the Worse

It was Saturday, New Year's Day, 1972. I was sick in bed with an ulcer. We were at our home in Bedford for the holidays, away from it all for ten days.

Frank had taken Eliot and Cristina to a nearby orchard to buy some apples and cider. It was an outing the children had been looking forward to for weeks.

I stayed in bed with my knees pulled up to my chest, trying to ease the pain. I was dizzy from the medication, and my mouth was dry.

My sister Susan was visiting us that weekend. She had come with her boyfriend. She came running into the room about ten o'clock and began to shake me violently. "Pat, wake up, wake up, the police are here. They want to see you."

"Police—what for?" I put on my robe and slowly negotiated my way downstairs. I had to hold on to the bannister to make it. A policeman was waiting outside the front door.

"Can I help you?" I asked.

"Mrs. Fernandez, your husband has been in an accident down the road. His car hit the stone abutment under Route 684."

"Oh my God," I gasped. "The children—what about the children? Are they all right? Is my husband all right?"

He answered quickly and assuredly, "The children are all right. Your husband is bleeding from the mouth, but an ambulance is already on the way. You have time to dress, Mrs. Fernandez. I'll wait for you and drive you to his car."

"Yes, yes, of course. Please come in." I swung the door open and ran toward the stairs. The dizziness was gone now. Once in my room, I pulled on my sweater and blue jeans. "Oh God, please let everything be all right," I prayed softly. "Don't let anything happen to any of them, please God."

Susan came in and said, "I'll watch Eric while you're gone. Please try to calm down."

I ran down the stairs, right past the policeman, and straight into the patrol car. The scene of the accident was only about five minutes away from the house, but it seemed as though it took us hours to get there.

As we approached the scene, I could see our car crumpled like an accordion against the abutment. As soon as the police car stopped, I jumped out and ran over to the accident. Eliot and Cristina were in the back seat, covered with a blanket. They were shivering, and their faces were white with the shock. Frank was in the front seat, blood coming from his mouth.

"The ambulance will be here in a few minutes," I said to Frank. "Try not to move. I love you. Please be OK."

His voice was just a whisper. "Don't worry about me. How are the children?"

"They're fine. They're in the back seat."

"Take them out of the car—not good for them."

I turned to one of the policemen. "My husband wants the kids taken out of the car. What do you think?"

"We'll put them in my car. I'll take them to the hospital after the ambulance comes."

I didn't know where I belonged. I wanted to be with both my husband and the children at the same time. When the ambulance finally arrived, the attendants placed Frank on a stretcher very gently. He sensed my confusion. "I'll be OK," he said. "The kids need you. Stay with them."

Mrs. Ellis, our housekeeper, arrived just as the ambulance door closed. The police had called her. She had been with us for years. She accompanied me in the police car to the hospital. I held Cristina close and rocked her gently on my lap. I held Eliot close with my other arm. "Daddy's going to be OK," I tried to assure them. I held them and sang the little songs I had written for each of them when they were born. *I must be strong,* I thought. *I must be strong for everyone.*

When we arrived, the children were taken to the emergency room. The ambulance had arrived there before us, and Frank was already inside. The tension increased, and my breathing became more and more labored. The sounds coming from my throat were strange. A nurse came over and gave me an injection. "Here, this will make you feel better," she said. "But you have to try and help yourself relax."

The children had bumps on their heads and lay still on the examination tables. Frank was complaining of pains in his chest. "I think I need a bone specialist," he said. "I think I have some broken ribs."

The hours passed in panic. Frank was moved to the intensive care unit, and they made me wait several hours before I could go in and see him. I wasn't prepared for what I saw. He was connected to a heart monitoring machine and had tubes going in and out of his nose. "What is that noise?" he asked.

"It's a machine of some sort. Don't let it bother you. Try

to relax. I was told that you shouldn't be here more than a couple of weeks, so don't worry. Everything is going to be fine. I love you so much. The kids love you. Just relax and get better."

I was scared when I saw that the tubes going in and out of him were filled with blood, but I didn't want to pass my fear on to him. He held my hand. "I want you to go home with the children. They need you more than I do right now." His voice was getting weaker and weaker.

"OK, but I'll be back to see you." I kissed his hand and his forehead. "I love you."

"I know you do," he said. "Now go home."

On my way out, I remarked to one of the nurses that I thought that blood going in and out of the tubes was wrong.

"Are you a doctor?" she snapped back.

"No, but it just seems strange."

"Look, you leave the nursing to us and go home. Your husband needs rest."

When Mrs. Ellis and the children and I left the hospital, it was already dark. Waiting for us at home were our attorney, Byron, and his wife, Debby.

"Pat, we heard. How is Frank?" Byron asked.

"I don't know. They said he should be home in about two weeks, but I don't know. He doesn't look good to me."

I was emotionally exhausted. Everyone tried to offer me reassurance. I fed the children dinner and then excused myself for the evening. "Pardon me, but I'm going to take the children up to bed and lie down with them," I said. "I think they're going to need a lot of hugging."

"Mrs. Fernandez, your husband has taken a turn for the worse." I had only been with the children for an hour when the call came from the hospital. The doctor sounded very evasive. "Could you please come down? We would like to talk to you about it. Do you have someone who could drive you?"

His words echoed through me—"taken a turn for the worse." My husband's personal secretary, Maria, and her husband, Jose, had also come over. I walked into the living room and gave them the news. "The doctor said that he's taken a turn for the worse. That means he's dead."

"Pat, that's not necessarily true," Byron said.

"I heard those words years ago. I know what they mean." I sobbed as I reached for my jacket.

"Mrs. Ellis has gone. Jose and I will take you to the hospital," Maria said. As we drove, Maria tried to reassure me.

"You don't understand. No one understands," I cried. "The words the doctor used. They mean Frank's dead, he's dead! Why don't you listen to me?"

Once we got to the hospital, we took the elevator straight up to the intensive care unit. As we ascended, I watched the floor indicators light up. "Turn for the worse—" I had lived this moment before.

The doctor was waiting for us as we got off. Beads of sweat rested on his forehead and above his upper lip.

"Mrs. Fernandez, come with me." He motioned us to a room at the end of a long corridor. I told Maria to stay where she was, that I wanted to do this alone.

"Please sit down, Mrs. Fernandez."

"No, I'd rather stand. What about my husband? I want to know."

"We did everything we could. We—" He fumbled with his hands as though he were at a loss for words.

"Is he dead?"

"Yes, I'm afraid so." The doctor's voice seemed to come from a distance. I only heard parts of sentences: "Died . . . you need . . . tranquilizer. . . ."

"I want to leave." I opened the door. All of a sudden I heard wailing through the corridor, "Nooo, nooo." My voice sounded far away. I kept crying out, "You don't understand. No one understands. I loved him. I loved him. I loved him."

I don't recall the rest of that evening very well. Everyone felt grief at his death. I sat and cried for hours and wouldn't let anyone get near me. No one could say anything to comfort me. I was positive that no one could understand the grief I was feeling. But I didn't have the words to tell anyone. All I could do was cry.

Maria and Jose agreed to spend the night at the house. "We have to take down the Christmas tree," Maria said. I think they were just looking for something to do to take their minds off things. As Maria and Susan started to take the tree down, I went upstairs so that I could hold the children close to me.

I didn't sleep. I held the children and thought of all the things I could have done for Frank, but didn't. I should have spent more time with him at work. I should have. I spoke to him as though he were in the room with me. "I'll make it up to you," I said. "I promise, I promise."

20

A Liberated Woman

Eliot, Cristina, and Eric came to the breakfast table. They were all strangely silent, as if they knew something was wrong.

I reached across the table to where Eliot and Cristina were sitting. "Give me your hands," I said to them. They all reached out and put their hands in mine. "I have something to tell you. It is something very sad and unhappy." I choked back the tears. "Your daddy is dead."

"Yes, Mommy, but when is he coming back?" Cristina asked.

"He's not coming back. Daddy died. He's all gone."

Eric banged on his high chair. He didn't understand. Eliot lowered his head and cried. "We have to be strong for Daddy," I said. "We have to stay close and help each other."

Eric banged his cookie on the high chair. I reached over and stroked his head and kissed his hand. "We're all going to miss Daddy very much."

The funeral and burial were simple and unadorned. My sisters, brother, and stepfather attended and were very supportive of me and the children. It took a tragedy to bring us together.

The day after the funeral, the vice-president of the

bakery called and demanded an employment contract and more money, threatening that he would quit. I knew I had to return to the office. The first day back I felt skittish, as though I had to learn the whole business over again from scratch. Byron, our attorney, accompanied me. I sat in my usual seat in Frank's office.

"Pat," Byron said, "you're going to have to take Frank's place from now on. Go over and sit behind the desk."

"I can't. It's not right. He belongs there, not me."

"Pat, you have to. Frank groomed you for this job. He always had a great deal of confidence in your ability to manage things for him. That's why he pushed you so much." Byron took me by the elbow and guided me toward the chair.

"I feel like an impostor. I don't belong here. I'm only twenty-eight."

"You can do it. Frank knew that."

"There are over a hundred employees here, mostly men. They all have families depending on us for money. That's a big responsibility."

"Then I guess you better get busy."

It was going to be hard to live up to Frank's expectations and fill the enormous void his passing left in my life. To fill it, I fell back on my panacea, work—as many hours as I could possibly fit into each day.

A New York bank and I were made executors of my husband's $3 million estate. Through a direct bequest, I received the house in New York City, plus the home in Bedford Hills and a beach house on Long Island. The rest of the will indicated that I was to receive $1 million. The remainder of the estate was to be divided equally between our three children and Peter and his sister.

The bank wanted me to handle the bakery exclusively. I didn't want to. No one in the family wanted to. Finally it was decided that I would assume the responsibility after I removed all building code violations from the real estate properties and refinanced the buildings so that they could be turned over to a management company. That would enable me to spend my entire time working on expanding the bakery.

The board of directors of the company elected me president and chairman of the board at a salary of sixty thousand dollars a year. I resolved to succeed, to make Frank proud of me. Throughout all my business dealings, I would try to please him.

I was filled with guilt for all the arguments Frank and I had had over my desire to stay away from the office. Several weeks after his death, I lined the walls of the sitting room of our New York City home with pictures of him. I would talk to him as though he were there. Even when I attempted to pray, my thoughts ultimately turned to Frank. "I'll prove to you that you didn't waste your time with me. I'll prove it, I'll prove it. You just watch." I'd even ask Frank to guide me in certain situations.

To boost the sales of the bakery, I hired a public relations firm to get our name known.

Tensions developed between Peter and me over the way I ran the business. We'd sit down and talk things out fairly often, but our attempts at reconciliation proved futile. He did not want to be an officer of the company.

I wanted to ship our product to other states. I wanted to fulfill Frank's dreams for the plant; but I had some dreams of my own that needed fulfilling as well.

We entered our products at the national motel and hotel show and won first prize for commercial bakeries, a prize that had usually gone to our competitors. As a result, we started to pick up accounts in other states.

I did not receive the support of the vice-president in any of my efforts. It became apparent that we were working against each other. After a meeting with the executors, it was decided that he should be replaced. I knew Frank would have wanted it that way.

Despite all the inner turmoil, my efforts were getting some attention in the press. *U.S. News and World Report* called me "New York's youngest lady tycoon." *Business Week* wrote, "A bakery thrives under her control." Other stories appeared in the *New York Times* and the *Wall Street Journal*.

The stories were an asset, both to the business and to my ego. An image was being created. I began to believe my press clippings. The time spent between myself and my children was limited. I saw them in the mornings and on weekends. At a time when they had to deal with the loss of their father, they had a governess to comfort them, not their mother.

Because of the trouble between Peter and me, I was forced to fire him. Company morale was really low because of the division, and firing him was necessary. I knew what other people in the company would think, namely, that I was trying to grab all the corporate power for myself, but that didn't matter. I had a timetable to keep. Frank would have wanted it that way.

It wasn't long before I began to equate personal worth with monetary worth. I was becoming a carbon copy of Frank. Though I covered my loss with work, I desperately needed friendship. The friends Frank and I had as a couple were also couples. But I was no longer a couple, and their calls for visits tailed off to nothing.

I developed new friends, however, friends who had read my clippings and clung to me for what I could do for them. But I blindly accepted them, not because I wanted to, but because I needed to. I needed friendship, even if it was only a facade.

By the world's standards, I had everything. I was rich, young, and successful. I was considered a liberated woman. I considered myself a liberated woman, and I was—liberated to a new bondage.

21

If There is Love, it Will Work

About a year after Frank's death, we moved to a new home closer to work. I wanted to get away from everything that reminded me of him.

Several months after the move, I decided to have the home partially renovated. I called one of the Greek carpenters, Tom, who had done some work in our other buildings. During the renovation, the carpenter had a visit from his brother, Hercules, a captain in the Greek merchant marine. Hercules was on leave in New York and decided to use his time in helping his brother work on my house.

Hercules was very attractive. We didn't speak much, but I enjoyed the few words we had together. He spoke and acted differently from the other Greek men his brother brought in to work from time to time. He was also an excellent cabinet maker. One afternoon while I was home for lunch, I was able to strike up a little conversation with him. "Hercules," I asked, "if you've been at sea so long, when did you have the time to learn how to do such beautiful work?"

"I learn from my stepfather as boy."

"Your stepfather?"

"Yes."

"What happened to your father?"

"After the Nazis leave my country at end of war, Communists come in and take over. My father work for government railroad. Communists did not like his political views. One day they come and take him away from his job and shoot him."

"How horrible! You were only children."

"Yes, but my mother marry again."

"Are you and your brother, Tom, from the same father?"

"Yes, but I have another brother in Greece. His name is Cristo. He is from my stepfather." Hercules continued working as he spoke. He was always the first to arrive on the job and the last to leave.

One day I came home from work to have lunch with the children. Hercules, Tom, and an older Greek gentleman were having lunch over by the staircase. They were all talking enthusiastically—each man waved his arms around so the others would understand the intensity of his feelings. The only word I understood from their conversation was "American." After I made sandwiches for the children, I walked over and invited myself into their conversation. "What are you saying about Americans?"

We are talking about American women and men and if they should marry Greeks," Tom said.

"Oh, I see. And what was the consensus?"

"Greek men should not marry American women."

"And what about Greek women?"

"That doesn't matter," the older man interjected.

"That doesn't make sense. Why should it be all right for a Greek woman to marry an American man, but not all right for a Greek man to marry an American woman?"

"Because American women are too independent," Tom said.

"Well, I think there's too much of a cultural difference. One thing is for sure: I'd never marry a Greek man."

"Why?" Hercules asked. It was the first time he had said anything.

"I heard that all Greeks and Italians want their women to be barefoot and pregnant. Besides, I want to be able to choose what I want to do. If I want to work, I don't want to be told I can't. I want to be able to decide for myself."

"If people love each other, things will work out," Hercules added.

"What does that mean? If a women loves a man, she will obey everything he says and then it will work out for him? What about the women?"

"If there is love, it will work. People grow together," Hercules said.

"That doesn't sound Greek to me. It doesn't even sound Spanish. I don't even hear American men talk like that." Hercules put his pipe between his teeth and smiled. He stood out from the rest—by a mile.

I was unable to get him out of my mind. I found myself coming home for lunch more often so that I'd be able to see him and maybe talk for a few minutes. I started leaving for work later in the morning and getting home earlier in the evening, just to get an extra look.

I had forgotten where, but I remembered that I had once read that in some areas of Greece, people still arranged the marriages of their children. In the absence of a parent, a brother or sister could be approached. *Do I dare?* I asked myself. *It sounds so primitive, yet there is something very modern about a woman proposing to a man, which is what I'd really be doing.*

One afternoon my mother's sister (whom I really didn't know that well) dropped by for lunch. I rushed her upstairs as soon as she walked in the front door and told her excitedly of my idea. I asked her if she would approach Tom and speak to him. She was startled. "You mean *propose?*" she asked.

"Yeah, Rosemary, propose. Why not? That's the way they do it in Greece."

"Are you sure? I think I'll feel a bit foolish trying to do this."

"Don't worry. Tom's really easy to get along with. Anyway, it won't reflect on you at all. He just might think that I'm a little crazy."

"All right, if that's what you want. I'll speak to him tonight."

"Good, now don't say anything to anyone."

That evening Aunt Rosemary called with some news.
"Did you ask him?" I asked.
"Yes," Rosemary said.
"Well, what happened?"
"Tom said he would tell Hercules tomorrow, when he sees him at work."
"Tomorrow? Wasn't Hercules there?"
"No, he's not staying in the same apartment."
"Oh, well thanks a lot. I hope I'll have some good news for you very soon."
"Maybe so. I still think this is a little crazy."

The next morning, as I came down the stairs I glanced over at Hercules. The expression on his face when he looked at me indicated he had not yet heard from his brother. That didn't matter—I still blushed.

"Would you like some coffee?" I asked.

"I love coffee. Thank you."

"I'll make some, then." The children ran down the stairs and into the kitchen. "Sit down and I'll make you some breakfast."

"I want some cereal, Mommy," Eric said.
"I want pancakes," Eliot countered.
"I want French toast," said Cristina.
"Well, guess what you're getting?" I said.
"What?"
"Eggs and toast and fruit. This isn't a restaurant. Hercules, have you had breakfast?"
"Yes."
"Are you sure? Can I make you something?"
"No thank you. Only coffee, please."

When I gave Hercules his coffee, he took it and started to walk into the next room. "No, please stay. Sit down with us." I waved to him to come back over.
"Are you sure?"
"Yes, please join us."

As soon as he sat down, I was speechless. I had no idea of what to say to him. Thank goodness for the children; they did some of the talking. Hercules told them about the ships he had been on, and the children asked him question after question.

The doorbell rang, and I gratefully bolted from the table to answer it. It was the old Greek man who worked with Tom and Hercules. I let him in, and he went straight to work. I went back to the kitchen and saw Hercules getting up from the table. He thanked me for the coffee and smiled. I blushed again. *This is ridiculous*, I thought. *I feel just like a schoolgirl.*

The governess came downstairs, and I said good-bye to the children. I walked out the door, still feeling childish and a bit flushed, but no less serious in my intentions.

That afternoon at work I felt sick. I decided to go home and rest for a while. When I arrived at the house, I saw that Hercules had spoken to Rosemary. I giggled and ran up the stairs. My stomach was really upset now. I flopped into my bed without undressing and pulled a small blanket over myself.

A few minutes later I heard Rosemary's voice followed shortly by some footsteps. She walked into my room without knocking.

"What's the matter?"

"I don't feel well."

"What's the matter? Did you speak to Hercules?"

"Not since I've been home. I really feel sick."

"He knows, you know."

"I thought so."

"He wants to talk to you."

"Now?"

"Now is just as good a time as any. Stay here. I'll tell him you don't feel well."

"Ohh, what am I going to say?"

"You'll thing of something," Rosemary answered as she walked out.

About five minutes later, I heard footsteps coming up the stairs again. "Hello?" It was Hercules.

I pulled the blanket up over my face. I heard him walk toward me. He pulled up a chair and sat down at the side of the bed. "What is this I hear from old man and Rosemary?"

Not uncovering my face, I asked, "Did Tom tell you?"

"No, old man told me something. I didn't believe him. Now Rosemary says something. It's true?"

"Yes," I said through the blanket.

"Only I will arrange my marriage," he said.

I finally pulled the blanket off my face. I wanted to hear what he had to say. Maybe I'd gotten him angry.

"It would be difficult for me—for us," he said. "We have different ways."

"I know that. But you said that if two people love each other it would work out."

"Yes, but I have no job here in America. I help Tom now because I am here. Tom does not need me."

"It doesn't matter. You can start your own business. I can help you."

"What about language? I do not speak well English."

"You could learn."

"Listen. Every day I watch you go and come home. I come early in morning to see you. I wait late to see you. I feel much for you. Still, it is very difficult. Are you sure you like to get married?"

"Yes," I put my hands over my face an peeked out through my open fingers. I couldn't believe I was acting this way.

"OK," he said, "let's get married."

"You mean it?" I jumped from the bed and threw my arms around him. We both laughed and ran downstairs.

That night Hercules and I had our first date, accompanied by his brother and his sister-in-law. We had a whirlwind courtship and were married ten days later in a Greek Orthodox church. We were planning on taking a two-week trip to Florida, but we were cut short by all the calls coming in from the office and the executors of Frank's will.

There were many problems in the marriage from the start. For one, Hercules was right about the cultural differences. They were a big problem. I had many luncheon appointments, most of them with other men, and Hercules could not understand what lunch had to do with business. I could not understand why he could not understand. Sometimes, in an attempt to ease his mind, I'd invite him to join me for some of the appointments, but it made both of us feel uneasy.

My salary was sixty-thousand dollars a year, plus expenses. Hercules often did not make as much in a week as I was used to spending for an evening out.

Though Frank was dead, I was still married to him emotionally, and I compared everything Hercules did to the way I thought Frank would have done it.

Hercules was generally very patient, understanding, and loving, however, and we earnestly tried to work things out. When I'd come home from work, I'd type up his bills, write out estimates for him, and generally try to guide him in how to conduct his business. And there was one thing that really helped make the marriage work: the children loved him immediately, and he took to them just as quickly.

We found it very difficult to live with each other, and yet we didn't want to be apart. Sometimes we would separate for a day, but we'd end up together the next day. Our marriage was off and on. Finally, after four months, we flew to Santo Domingo, in the Dominican Republic, and got a quick divorce. The day after the divorce, we were back together again. I couldn't understand how you could love someone and yet not be able to live with him, but then when you were apart, not be able to live without him.

22

Elusive Peace and Rest

It wasn't long before I realized I couldn't handle the pressures of a demanding business, children who needed me, and an off-again, on-again relationship. I was being tugged at from all directions.

The bakery business in the United States was not prospering in the early 1970's. People were merging, selling out, or closing down. Times were getting rough for my business as well. Our profits were being eaten up by rising labor and material costs, and I was torn between being married to my business or being married to my family.

I was on the verge of a nervous breakdown. *What would Frank think of this?* I asked myself. I wanted desperately to be free from the bakery business. I also wanted to please my late husband and be with my family, all at the same time.

I met with the executors of the estate and told them I hoped they would be able to find a buyer for the bakery. I was at my wits' end.

Prospective buyers were brought to the bank. Nothing worked out. Then I thought that Peter would like it as part of his share in the estate. I mentioned the possibility to the bank. They later contacted Peter, who declined the offer.

"I can't stay on too much longer," I told Byron. "I'm getting too sick. My ulcers are acting up daily; I'm living in constant pain. My family needs me, and I want my realtionship with Hercules to work out. I can't be at the bakery all day and then come back every night to check production and worry about estate matters and everything else. If we can't find a buyer for the business, let the bank put in someone to take my place. I'll resign."

Several months later I did resign, but the bank refused to accept the resignation. Eventually, however, the company that Peter worked for, a rival bakery, offered to buy me out. The day of the contract signing, I sat in one of the large offices of the bank's headquarters. I waited as the bank and its attorneys and myself and my attorneys went over each word. I sat doubled over in pain. The very moment I signed the papers, I got up to leave, but I couldn't stand by myself. The pain shot through my stomach and up my back. One of the attorneys for the bank helped me out of the office. The buyers—our competition—were waiting outside to sign their papers. I couldn't look them in the face. Everything I had worked for had crumbled. I was a failure. Frank would never have let this happen.

The attorney escorted me down to the main floor, where Hercules was waiting. I was surprised to see him, but also relieved. "You're always there when I need you," I said.

"What happened?" he asked.

"My ulcer—I couldn't take it—letting go, that is. Peter was smart. He must have known this thing was a monster, a monster that consumes."

We sold our house in the city and moved out to the home in Bedford Hills. The children would be starting school, and I wanted them to have good environment to learn and grow in.

There were so many changes going on that I found it difficult to adjust. I had no peace; I didn't know who or what to blame. Personal medical problems only compounded the worries. Shortly after the move, I had to go to the hospital for a partial hysterectomy. After the surgery, I became extremely nervous, and the doctor prescribed Valium to calm me down.

I thought I needed time to think and reflect, to get away from New York for a while. So during the Christmas break from school, I took the children down to Florida. Hercules, at that time, was working for a builder in Pennsylvania. After spending two weeks in Florida, I called Hercules and told him I wanted to go to Spain. His reply was gentle and understanding. All he said was, "I hope you find what you're looking for."

My friends Maria and Jose had been transferred to Spain because of Jose's job. They helped me find a two bedroom apartment in Madrid when I got there. The children slept in one room, and I slept in the other.

It was no different in Spain. The peace I was searching for seemed to elude me. It could not be found in a person. It could not be found in a place. I was unhappy even though I had everything the world thought was necessary for happiness. Though we were divorced, I still had Hercules, three wonderful children, plenty of money, and a beautiful home—two beautiful homes. But I had an emptiness inside me that ached.

The loneliness and despair grew worse. Though I learned to speak Spanish fairly well, my children were in a good English school, and I lived near Maria and Jose, I still felt alone.

Every day I went into the church near my apartment

and prayed. My prayers were often without words, just tears and an agonizing nagging and fighting from within. There was a missing link somewhere, and I knew it, but I was unable to figure out what it was.

I called Hercules and told him what was going on. I asked him if he could get time off from work and come join me in Spain. He was able to come, even though it meant he would lose a lot of income. His love and strength gave us all a sense of security. But something was still missing, something separating me from the peace and the rest I needed.

23

Back on the Road Again

When Hercules arrived in Spain, I poured out my feelings to him. I told him of the emptiness, of the struggle I was having with a force that I thought was unknown to me.

"Don't worry," he said, "I know you will find what you are looking for."

"How do you know that?"

"Because you want it very badly."

"Well, I hope you're right, but it would help if I knew what it was."

We remained in Spain for several days after Hercules arrived, and then we decided to rent a car and drive to Greece to meet his mother and stepfather, both of whom I had never met. They did not know yet that Hercules and I were divorced.

When we arrived in Athens, we took two hotel rooms near the airport. The next day we went and surprised Hercules' mother. With tears in her eyes, she greeted her son and spoke to me with the only English words she knew. She hugged me and said. "Patricia, my Patricia," over and over. She smiled at me with such love and affection that I thought I would burst. The children ran to her and hugged her all at the same time. They, too, sensed the genuine affection of this lovely Greek woman.

Grandmother in Greek is "Ya Ya," and grandfather is "Pa Pous." Ya Ya and Pa Pous insisted that we stay with them during our visit. They also insisted that we take their room.

The most important thing I learned in Greece was the necessity of having a loving family to support you. I knew that I really needed this. Hercules' family had a closeness that I didn't think could be matched anywhere. How I wanted to be a part of it.

I learned more about love and caring and sharing in the ten days we spent in Greece than I had in my entire life. Hercules' mother, though she spoke no English, taught me so much by the example of her life. She prayed daily for us and for her son Tom and his family back in America.

When we returned to the United States, we went directly to Pennsylvania and stayed the remainder of the summer, until Hercules finished his work.

When we returned to Bedford Hills, we were married again. Hercules went to work, the children attended school, and I was at home, trying to be the perfect housewife. I found, however, that my house cleaned quickly, the shopping was done early, and the rest of the day I paced back and forth like a caged animal.

Friends I knew from my business days would call and ask how I was doing. Eventually the conversation would always turn to what I was doing *now*.

"Oh, taking it easy. I haven't decided what to do. Maybe I'll try my hand at being a travel agent."

Sometimes my friends would encourage me to go into real estate in the country; they wanted me to start my own business.

The longer I stayed out of work, the more I began to lose confidence in my abilities. Apart from cleaning, cooking, and picking up after my family, I had no idea at all what my purpose in life was supposed to be.

I mulled over a lot of options such as taking art classes, pottery classes, or dancing classes, but I didn't really know where to begin.

I had no awareness of God's presence in my life, because I was trying to live my life independent of Him. Nevertheless, His plan for me was operative in all those years of turmoil, providing for me and preserving me. He was working out His grace in practical, down-to-earth ways. And He was able to use even my most difficult experiences to bring me back to Himself.

A casual acquaintance invited me to visit the pastor of his church. He also related to me how Christ had come in to his life and totally changed it. I told him about my experience at the Billy Graham crusade years ago, and how I thought I had made a decision back then but had since fallen away. This man sensed my turmoil and knew that I needed my life changed.

I didn't take him up on his offer immediately. One day, however, in desperation, I called a nearby church and made an appointment to see the pastor. For a reason unknown to me, the appointment had to be canceled. So I called my friend and agreed to see the minister of his church. The appointment was made, and the next morning I arrived at the Christian and Missionary Alliance Church in nearby Armonk, New York. The minister had been held up on his way back from a meeting because of car trouble. As I waited, I spoke to his secretary, a woman named Barbara Murley. She listened to me a lot and from time to time would ask a question. She told me about the love of Christ, but it didn't penetrate. My ears heard her, but I was deaf to her words.

After two hours I left. The pastor had still not shown up.

Off and on throughout our marriage, Hercules had expressed a desire to go back to Greece. One day I suggested to him that it might not be such a bad idea. "Do you think you would be happy there?" Hercules asked.

"Why not. It would be a new adventure and experience. And besides, I really love your family."

The very next day we started making arrangements.

24

Dreams and Visions

On our way to give our car to the shippers, we stopped at a convenience store. I looked for a paperback I could read on the plane. I spun the rack around and glanced at the titles. Nothing I saw appealed to me. Then, as an afterthought, I decided to buy some science fiction. There were a few selections to choose from on the top section of the rack.

I could see Hercules motioning for me to hurry up, so I reached out and grabbed a book I thought was science fiction. It was called *The Late Great Planet Earth*.

After rushing back to the car, I stuffed the book into a bag I planned to carry on the plane.

Our drive was a mixture of excitement and anticipation. We were thrilled that we were able to sell our house so quickly. Hercules wanted to go into business with his brother Cristo and open a furniture showroom in Greece. There was so much to be done. We planned to stay with Hercules' mother while we searched for an apartment. Then, after furnishing it, we planned to look for a store for Hercules and his brother to rent.

I was thrilled at having such a good father for the children. I kept reminding myself that there were not many men who would marry a woman with three children. Hercules was strong, yet kind and gentle. He was the support the children and I needed so badly.

But if I had so much, why was I so restless? Why was I unable to lay down roots anywhere? I didn't have an answer. All I knew was that I was unhappy.

The children were as excited about the trip as we were. They kept talking about Ya Ya and Pa Pous and telling Hercules and me how much they loved them.

The trip was smooth, marred only by Eliot's battle with air sickness. When we arrived in Athens, it didn't take us long to pass though customs. We were out in the waiting room within twenty minutes, and Cristo was waiting for us.

What an exciting moment it was to see the children run into Cristo's arms. As I watched them, I realized that this was the only real family they knew. And I realized that I, too, needed the warmth and security that his family offered.

My in-laws' house was very small. To provide places for everyone, the dining room had to be converted into a bedroom. And we had to adjust to the absence of many of the conveniences we take for granted in America.

Underneath, though, I knew this change in lifestyle wasn't at the root of what was bothering me. When I found that my restlessness was persisting, I attributed it to my frustration over cramped quarters and the difficulties involved in normally simple procedures such as taking a bath.

We found a lovely apartment just a few blocks from the Mediterranean. Hercules and his brother found a store to rent and opened up their showroom. The store was something they had both planned and saved for for years.

At last, I thought, *the perfect environment. No more stress of running a business; my husband is a good provider; we live near the ocean; we have a great family. Now everything will be all right.*

I didn't know how to speak Greek, but when I saw all those beautiful Greek gals with their winsome smiles talking to my husband, I decided I had better learn the language quickly. I signed up for a class that was held in Athens a few mornings each week. Within two months I was able to converse and understand people, as long as they spoke slowly.

The first few months in Greece were delightful. The children and I went swimming every day. The most exciting part of our week was Sunday, when our family and Hercules' family would spend the day driving through the countryside outside Athens. We would visit a few parks and then stop at a small restaurant for coffee and pastry. By late afternoon we would come home, and everyone would take a nap while dinner was cooking in the oven.

Everything was rosy. The children loved the American community school. Their friends were children from several different countries, and they would discuss with our children experiences of what it was like to live and grow up in their country. This was a much better way of learning about culture than reading it in a book. I loved living in Greece with my family.

Then something started tearing me apart inside. At night I began having terrible nightmares that would frighten me. Some of those dreams even came true. I dreamed of planes crashing, and the next day a plane would come down. I dreamed that my mother-in-law had a heart attack, and that very week she did. One day Hercules was standing near the glass door in our apartment, and I screamed at him, "Get away! Get away! The door is going to break!" I was frantic, and he stepped back because he had seen some of my premonitions come true before. Just as he stepped back, the glass shattered.

These dreams and premonitions were about to drive me crazy. I didn't know where this ability was coming from, and I didn't want any part of it. I would often wake up crying because I had had a dream and was scared it was going to come true. I was surrounded by love from my family, and I was in the perfect environment, yet I felt a terrible oppression that was growing every day. There were days when I felt like driving my car into a wall. Sometimes I would lie on the bed, crying, and Hercules would ask me what was wrong. I wasn't able to tell him, because I didn't know myself.

One evening, about six months after we had arrived in Greece, Hercules' family came over to watch television. I didn't feel like concentrating on the language, so I looked around for something to read. I couldn't find anything in English other than the few magazines I had already read. Then I remembered the book I had bought at the convenience store before we left the United States. I thought it was a science fiction thriller and would provide a good change of pace.

As I read, I couldn't believe what the book was saying. A few days later, I made a trip into Athens to a book shop that sold English titles. I purchased a Bible to see if what this Lindsey was saying was true. For the next few weeks, I searched and searched the Scriptures. I told my kids some of the things I was discovering. I began to pray in earnest for the first time in years. While I prayed, however, the dreams and the oppression actually became worse.

I realized that I had to made a choice. Lindsey's book didn't make it clear just what kind of a decision was necessary for me or what choices I had. One of the things that did come through was that I should seek out an evangelical church and look into the Bible for answers to problems with my life.

One day I sat down with Hercules and tried to explain some of what I was experienceing.

"Honey, I want you to understand what's happening to me. I know that sounds ridiculous, because you've been so understanding all along. But I feel as though I'm at a turning point."

"Go on, go on. Tell me."

"I'm really mixed up. I'm frightened about the dreams and visions I've been having. I don't know how to handle it. Sometimes I want to kill myself just to get some relief from the oppression I feel. Then there are other times when I feel that I need to get to know God much better. But I don't know how to do that." I started to cry. Hercules put his arm around my shoulder and held me close. I sat up straight.

"You've been so patient all this time. You've given me the freedom to search out what I've been looking for. But there's still something wrong. Will you give me the freedom to go back to the United States? I have the feeling that I might find some answers in an evangelical church. From what I understand, they are Bible-believing and really know the Scriptures and where to find the answers. But maybe they don't. Maybe what I need is a psychiatrist. I just know that if I don't get some help soon, I'm going to fall apart."

"I don't know why you have to go back to United States to find answers, but if you have to, you have to. I only want what is the best for you."

"I know. I really know that." He held me in his arms for a long time.

25

I'm Talking About Submission

The Christmas holiday had passed, and the new year of 1976 was drawing near. With the new year always came the memory of my late husband. And now it was only a short time before the children and I left for New York again.

My mother-in-law was tearful nearly every time I saw her. She feared there was something terribly wrong between Hercules and myself. She could not understand why I was returning to the United States without him. Hercules and I tried to reassure her that everything was going to be all right. We tried to convince her that our marriage was not in trouble. And, in fact, it wasn't.

I was in trouble. I understood this, and so did Hercules. But Hercules had known all along that one day it was all going to work out, and then everything would be fine. He was able to see deep within me, and though I was sure he couldn't understand anything I was going through, he actually understood everything. I don't know how, but he did.

The children and I boarded the plane, and they shouted to Hercules, "Hurry up and finish your work, Daddy, and come and see us." Hercules and I hugged each other very tight. Neither of us wanted to let go.

While sitting on the plane, I was a mixture of fear and

dread. I felt like an emotional volleyball. But I knew that I must once and for all earnestly seek the God I had searched for all those years. I also knew that there were a psychiatrist and a mental hospital waiting if I didn't make the connection. I just knew that something had to happen, one way or the other.

We arrived in New York on a Sunday afternoon and stayed at a motel close to where we used to live. I called the real estate woman who had sold our house for us and asked if she knew of an evangelical church in the area. She mentioned Hillside Church in Armonk, the same church where I had talked so long with the secretary. She got in touch with the church for me.

Someone from Hillside called me and arranged for another person to pick up me and the children and take us to the evening service.

That night I heard people give testimonies of how Jesus had changed their lives, how He was continually working to make them into whole people. I also spoke to the secretary, Barbara Murley, after the service. Even though it had been two years since we had spoken, she still remembered me.

I don't remember anything that Barbara Murley or anyone else said to me in the following weeks. I don't even remember what the minister taught. I do remember that I cried a great deal.

Barbara called me every day. I don't remember exactly what we discussed, but she directed me to portions of Scripture that dealt with my problems.

One of the passages had to do with submission:

Wives, be subject to your husbands, as to the Lord. For the husband is the head of the wife as Christ is the head of the church, his body, and is himself its Savior. As the church is subject to Christ, so let wives be subject in everything to their husbands [Eph. 5:22-24].

This particular passage kept getting stuck in my throat. Submission to my husband meant dependence, which meant there was a chance I could get hurt. I didn't like that. The thought of submitting to anyone else was terrifying to me. It didn't matter that I was doing a lousy job of being independent. The verses scared me, so I chose to discard them, for the moment.

Then I started to learn about commitment. That was something I had never heard of before. I had heard about surrendering one's life to Christ, but I had never heard about commitment. It was like a puzzle; there were lots of little pieces, but I wasn't sure where any of them went or what kind of picture they made.

I began to search the Scriptures again. There were moments when they offered me great comfort, and there were moments when they corrected me. I was hungry, and I knew that everything else I had tried in life had failed miserably. I continued to read and pray.

I was so hungry to read God's Word that I spent most of my waking hours in the Scriptures. When the children left for school, I was sitting at the table, reading. While they watched television, I kept on reading. After they went to bed, I went on reading.

I read Exodus and wondered why it was necessary for God's people to spend so much time in the wilderness. Then I realized that they were like me. God let them wander on their own until they realized that their own strength was insufficient. I was starting to realize that my own resources weren't worth much, either.

And just as Israel had forgotten how God had supplied them with food and water in time of need, so, I, too, had forgotten how many times God had come to my aid. I didn't even see my supply as coming from God, but instead depended upon myself.

I learned that God had pledged Himself to take care of us. This was a covenant relationship. God has said that He will be our God *if* we will be His people. The covenant is conditional.

One of the most enlightening portions of Scripture I read was Joshua 3:5: "And Joshua said to the people, 'Sanctify yourselves; for tomorrow the Lord will do wonders among you." I continued on to what became one of the most important revelations God was to show me, the story of Israel's crossing the Jordan into the promised land.

> So, when the people set out from their tents, to pass over the Jordan with the priests bearing the ark of the covenant before the people, and when those who bore the ark had come to the Jordan, and the feet of the priests bearing the ark were dipped in the brink of the water (the Jordan overflows all its banks throughout the time of harvest), the waters coming down from above stood and rose up in a heap far off, at Adam, . . . and the people passed over opposite Jericho. And while all Israel were passing over on dry ground, the priests who bore the ark of the covenant of the LORD stood on dry ground in the midst of the Jordan, until all the nation finished passing over the Jordan [Josh. 3:14–17].

I was impressed that *both feet* of the priests had to be in the Jordan before it would part. In other words, they had to walk in totally committed, knowing God would perform that which He had promised.

I recalled how many times I had called out to God, "Lord, Lord," and had laid my petition before Him. I had called Him Lord; I had one foot in. But the other foot was planted firmly in the world. God wanted me to offer myself to Him in whole-hearted commitment, freely, out of love, in response to His love for me.

I had to give in. I had done things my own way for too long, and I had paid dearly for it. I wanted to go home. I wanted part of the promised land. One morning at around three, I fell to my knees and cried. At first there was just a trickle, and then the tears came down in a torrent. "God," I cried, "I don't understand why it has to be this way. I don't understand why I have to submit. I don't understand. I can't even agree with a lot of the things You say. But I'm willing to learn and do it Your way, no matter what the cost."

I was truly sorry for grieving my Lord. "Jesus, forgive me and let me feel Your presence in my life, please," I said. After a while, a feeling of release came over me. I was still crying, but the tears were tears of joy. A peace came over me that cannot be explained, only experienced.

I had found the missing link, Jesus. Only through Him could I come to the Father. He is a personal Messiah. I had spent my time in the wilderness that He might humble me and test me.

I called Hercules immediately and told him that I had committed my life to the Lord.

26

A Sheep in the Midst of Wolves

"Doxa to Theo" (Praise be to God), said Hercules when I told him that I had met the Lord. Hercules told me he would sell his business and come back to us as fast as he could. It took him only two weeks to get things in order and return.

I felt as though scales had been lifted off my eyes, and I could see for the first time.

> But when a man turns to the Lord the veil is removed. Now the Lord is the Spirit and where the Spirit of the Lord is, there is freedom. And we all, with unveiled face, beholding the glory of the Lord, are being changed into his likeness from one degree of glory to another; for this comes from the Lord who is the Spirit [2 Cor. 3:16–18].

After the Lord freed me from bondage, things started to happen. First, I prayed a very special prayer that is still being answered. I prayed that the Lord would teach me to look only to Him as my source of supply, and that He would help me submit to my husband and recognize him as the head of our household.

"Good grief!" Have you ever heard that expression and wondered how grief could be good? Now I know.

There are some prayers that God answers immediately, and some He answers later. Either way, He knows when the time is right. My prayer for submission and dependence was going to be answered immediately, but not in the ways I expected.

The attorneys for Peter, my late husband's son, and his sister had petitioned the court to have me refund all money and property I had received from the estate as a direct bequest. They claimed that Frank, who had been the executor of Peter's mother's estate, had misused some of the funds, and they had been transferred to my estate.

What had once been a $3 million estate had now dwindled in value to a few hundred thousand dollars. The bank said this was due to the economy. I thought there were other reasons. The bank said they wanted my house and money to be returned to the estate to pay estate taxes. The government comes before the beneficiary.

I was served all kinds of legal papers. Most of the law firms I contacted wanted a great deal of money before they even began to work, plus a percentage of the settlement. Peter and his sister had some very good attorneys, and the bank had an army of them.

I spent many days in prayer about the situation. I knew that the "order to show cause" why I shouldn't be required to return the estate money and my home had to be answered. I had no lawyer. Who would represent me?

I had read in the book of Judges how God told Gideon to go down and fight the Midianites, and Gideon was afraid:

Pray, Lord, how can I deliver Israel?
Behold, my clan is the weakest in Manasseh,
and I am the least in my family [Judg. 6:15].

Gideon doubted himself and his own abilities. He might have even doubted his own sanity. He wasn't at all sure if this message was really from God.

I wondered if the Lord had been speaking to me through His Word. Like Gideon, I wondered if I wasn't going just a bit too far. *Could it be,* I wondered, *that the Lord might want me to go to court, using Him as my attorney?* All doors shut. No one would represent me.

I went through old records and files, sorting out the documents. I spread them out over the kitchen table and prayed to the Lord for guidance.

I knew I couldn't go down to court alone. Hercules couldn't go because of a job he was involved in. I called the minister of the Hillside Church, Dave Schroeder, and asked him if he would accompany me. He agreed.

We entered the courtroom. It would be a few minutes before all the parties would be called. While we were waiting, Dave gave me a passage of Scripture to read.

> Behold, I send you out as sheep in the midst of wolves; so be wise as serpents and innocent as doves. Beware of men, for they will deliver you up to councils. . . . When they deliver you up, do not be anxious how you are to speak or what you are to say; for what you are to say will be given to you in that hour; for it is not you who speak, but the Spirit of your Father speaking through you [Matt. 10:16–20].

The parties were called. The largest law firms in New York were representing the banks. The firm representing Peter also brought a couple of attorneys. We all went up before the judge, the attorneys, myself, and God. Above the judges seat there was a sign which read, "In

God We Trust." My knees shook as I stood in front of the judge and alongside the row of attorneys.

I presented the court with copies of my answer to the show cause order. I stated my case to the judge and the other attorneys. I made reference to the various documents I had attached to the answer. Then the attorneys for the other side spoke.

Finally, the judge turned to me and asked, "Miss, is your client present in court?"

"I am the client," I answered.

"Then which one of these gentlemen is your attorney?"

"I have no attorney, your honor. I will represent myself."

From that point on, everything was put on the record. I was not surprised when the judge ruled that I would not be allowed to sell the Bedford Hills property, and if I did, the money would be held in escrow, and I would not have access to it. Also, the funds for our Armonk house had to be held in escrow.

That really put a dent in our plans. We had put a down payment on another home when we returned from Greece and had planned to use the money from the sale of the Armonk home to close on the new house. The judge's order meant we would have no money to pay for the closing, and we would forfeit our deposit.

What happened in court does not sound like a great victory, but it was. For the first time in my life, I had stepped out and trusted God. I had asked Him to make me totally dependent on Him. God had answered that prayer and was now ready to teach me what faith is all about.

Hercules had put a deposit on a home just a few miles away from our previous one. This was the first time in our married life that he had purchased anything entirely with his own money and none of mine. But neither he nor I had enough money stashed away for the closing.

Then I thought of all the jewelry Frank had given me. I had had it appraised by a jeweler, who estimated its value at thirty-five thousand dollars. But then God showed me that I was looking to my own resources again, not to Him.

Hillside Church was having a building drive at this time. With Hercules' permission, I went to Dave Schroeder and gave him a large box filled with diamonds, rubies, emeralds, and pieces of gold jewelry. I gave it to the building fund. I also returned the Bedford Hills property to the estate, even though the count did not order it. I needed to be rid of all material possessions and stand alone with God, depending on Him as my source.

A few weeks later, the Lord provided for our need plus some additional money to see us through. The owners of an apartment building Hercules had renovated decided to pay us months before we had expected it.

Hercules put his trust in the Lord soon after this. He could see how faith was working in my life, and how the Lord provided for us throughout. Over a period of about a year, each of our children came to know the Lord as well. We had taken that all-important first step, the step of faith. It was a wobbly one, but it was made. The Lord was teaching us how to walk again.

God promised to bring His people into the promised land, a land that flowed with milk and honey. He didn't say, however, that there wouldn't be any giants there.

There were giants in our promised land, but we learned that our Lord is bigger than any of them. We had to trust Him.

Trusting was a lesson that our entire family had to learn. There were many times when it was tempting to take things into our own hands. Hercules was making about two hundred dollars a week. It was barely enough to make ends meet. Hercules knew that he could make more money eventually if he decided to do cabinet work and carpentry on his own, but he didn't know how long that would take. Nevertheless, on Christmas Eve, 1976, he quit his job with another builder and made plans to start on his own.

We advertised in a few Westchester County newspapers, not knowing what the response would be. By the end of January, Hercules was so swamped with work that he asked me if I could give him a hand. So, I rolled up my sleeves and went down to the basement with my husband to learn how to become a cabinet maker.

27

Another Lesson

It was a bright and beautiful summer Sunday morning in August 1977, the kind of day that makes you forget your troubles.

Cristina was sick in bed that day. Although we normally would have been on our way to church, I was headed to the drugstore for some medicine for my daughter. Hercules had decided to work on the house, because the rest of us were not going and he would have been uncomfortable by himself.

When I left for the drugstore, Hercules and his friend were working on the front of the house. Hercules was cutting a piece of redwood for some stairs he was making.

As I drove home from the pharmacy, I started to sing. There is just something about God's creation that makes me want to burst out in songs of praise to Him. When I pulled into the driveway, I didn't see Hercules or his friend Terry. Instead, I saw Eliot lying on the ground, pulling the grass out in clumps. He lifted his head, and I saw that his eyes were filled with tears. The dirt was smudged all over his face where he had wiped away the tears. Eric came tearing out of the house very excited and upset, which wasn't too unusual around our house. I thought that the two boys had just gotten into another fight.

"Where is your father? Does he know about this?"

Eliot, still trying to choke back the tears, blurted out another story. "It's about Daddy." He was really having trouble getting his words out. "Daddy cut his leg with the big saw, and his leg was all opened up and the muscles were hanging out. Look, see the saw? It has some blood on it. I don't want Daddy to die, Mommy. I don't want Daddy to die."

I tried to be calm. "Where is Daddy?"

"Terry took him to the hospital in his car."

I went in to see Cristina and give her the medicine. She was weak from the flu and thought the boys were just kidding her when they told her about Hercules. She said she had tried to call me at the pharmacy, but that I had already gone. I told her that I would get our neighbor to come over and watch her, and I would take the boys to the hospital.

I told Eliot and Eric to get into the car. I drove over to our neighbor's and told her what had happened. She said she would go over and watch Cristina.

We were heading for the same hospital we had taken Frank to five and half years earlier. Eliot couldn't keep from crying and crying. I tried to calm the boys by reciting some Scripture to them.

"Boys, do you remember what it says in Romans 8:28, that all things work together for good to those who love God and are called according to His purpose? God has brought us through a lot. Nothing can happen to any of us that He doesn't already know. God hasn't brought us this far to take Daddy away from us.

When we got to the hospital, I went straight to the emergency room. Hercules was in terrible pain and was waiting for a surgeon to arrive. I could only look at his leg for a few seconds before I had to turn away.

I cradled his head and waited with him until the surgeon came. After he had been wheeled inside, I ran to a phone in the corner of the waiting room and called our church. I spoke to Dave Schroeder just before the morning service was to begin and asked him if he would have the congregation pray for Hercules.

Hercules was in the emergency room for nearly three hours. When the doctor finished sewing up the leg, it was bandaged and we were told it was safe to take him home. I was surprised that they didn't keep him in for observation, but I didn't ask any questions.

The next couple of days, Hercules suffered from severe pain and a high fever. The doctor prescribed codeine and aspirin to keep the pain down. But Hercules continued to have trouble. The drugs didn't seem to be having any effect. He was restless, and the pain just kept getting worse. He would be feverish one minute and complain of chills the next.

Two days after the accident, I took Hercules back to the hospital. The doctor opened up the stitches to see if any infection had set in. I sat in the waiting room for nearly an hour before the doctor came in with the news. "Mrs. Assimakopoulos? I'm afraid we are going to have to admit your husband. I believe he has gas gangrene in his leg—it's possible he might lose it.

After Hercules was admitted, I went in to sit with him. "Did he tell you what might happen?" I asked him. "Did he tell you that you might lose your leg?" I was trying to be gentle, but how could anything like that sound gentle? I just didn't want Hercules to wake up one morning and suddenly discover what had happened to him without having had any warning. I prayed with him for strength for both of us. He closed his eyes.

It was vacation Bible school time, so I knew that the children would be taken care of during the mornings. The gracious people at our church and our assistant pastor, Carl von Stein, agreed to make arrangements for the children for the rest of each day.

Hercules had been placed in quarantine and hooked up to an intravenous feeding device. He was also being given massive doses of penicillin to combat the infection. He was allowed visitors as long as they were wearing hospital gowns, hair covers, and surgical masks.

A specialist was called in to examine Hercules. He told me that the next forty-eight hours would be very critical. How he responded to treatment would determine whether he had to be transferred to New York City.

I stayed all that day and evening with Hercules and attended to his needs. I slept that night in the chair in his room. Early the next morning, around seven o'clock, I went to check on him again. His skin had turned a pale yellowish orange during the night. I called the nurse, who quickly called the specialist. After the specialist did another examination, he said that Hercules would have to be moved to Mt. Sinai Hospital in the city and placed in a hyperbaric chamber, a sealed-off chamber that contains pure oxygen and is supposed to facilitate the healing process greatly. Hercules would be in a completely sterile environment. The doctor told me to hope for the best, the best being that Hercules would only lose his leg.

Once at Mt. Sinai, Hercules spent several hours in the chamber every day. And every day the doctors would come in and cut off a little more muscle. The rest of his time was spent in the intensive care unit.

We found out that Hercules has a rare blood type. When I took this concern before our church, I found that they participated in a blood bank program. It meant that if a member needed blood, it would be available.

I spent days, and sometimes nights, with Hercules. Often I would make two trips a day to the hospital from home so that I could spend some time with the children, too. They needed me. They were full of fears and anxieties that they couldn't reveal to anyone else.

One morning our associate pastor went with me to the hospital. He held my arm as one of the doctors spoke to me gently but frankly: "Mrs. Assimakopoulos, we are doing everything we can to save your husband's leg, but we must tell you at this point that we are more concerned with his life. It doesn't look too good."

28

Grace Upon Grace

I watched him deteriorate. I watched his weight drop until his bones threatened to cut through his skin. He was dying. The nurses in the intensive care unit got permission for the children to come in and see him. That wasn't regular practice.

When I brought the children, they put on the white gowns and pulled them up as they walked so they wouldn't trip over them. We got three chairs and placed them next to the bed so the children could climb up and reach over the restraining bars.

Hercules tried to smile. He was weak, but he tried to talk to the children and give them a little comfort. "I look like—like bionic man," he said. The strain was too great, and he started to cry.

Cristina reached over and grabbed a tissue from the table. She wiped Hercules' tears and then her own. "Don't be afraid," she said. "God is going to heal you, Daddy."

Eliot had trouble staying by the bed. He leaned over and whispered to me, "Mom, I can't stay. I can't see Daddy like this."

"OK," I said. "First, we'll all pray with Daddy, and then you can go outside."

We laid our hands on Hercules and began to pray. Each child took a turn praying, the three sweetest prayers I've ever heard. Each prayer indicated complete trust in the healing power of the Lord.

Eric held Hercules' hand and Christina, wiping his tears and her own, said, "Look Daddy, your tears and mine are together. I'm going to save this tissue and give it to you when you come home."

God said yes to our prayers. It was several weeks before Hercules was no longer in danger of losing his life, but I could detect even throughout that period that he was getting a little bit stronger. Three weeks after the children visited, he was moved out of the intensive care unit and into a private room. The doctors were still cutting bits of muscle off his leg, looking to see if the gangrene was spreading or had been arrested.

Each day when I visited, I read to him from the Bible. I also brought along cassette tapes of Christian music and of some of the sermons I had heard.

Dave Schroeder and I were at Hercules' bedside, praying over him, one afternoon. He had been in the hospital more than a month. As we finished praying, Hercules suddenly opened his eyes. "I saw Jesus Christ," he said. "Jesus said, 'Don't be afraid just follow Me.' Then he touched me."

"What, what are you talking about? How do you feel?" I asked.

"The pain is gone."

The doctors had not been able to sew up Hercules' leg because of the nature of the wound and the amount of muscle that had been removed, so they had just put tapes across it. But whenever they came and took the tape off, the wound would slide around like Jell-O. The morning after the pastor and I had prayed, the doctors came in to remove the tape and take some more muscle. Much to their surprise, the wound had healed shut.

"What happened?" one of the doctors asked.

"Jesus healed it." Hercules said. The doctors just stared at each other.

When God does a job, it's a great one, and that goes for His miracles. Whether large or small, they are all great.

Hercules spent about three more weeks in the hospital. He got back on solid foods and was learning how to use crutches. When the time came to go home, Hercules was treated to the most gorgeous fall I had ever seen. It was as though God had saved the colors, the good ones, just for Hercules.

While he was at home, he had to have a private nurse come over each day and change his bandages. After a couple of weeks at home, he was admitted to the Burke Rehabilitation Center in White Plains, New York, for a month. He had to learn how to walk again.

Shortly before he left the rehabilitation center, he was allowed to go to church one Sunday morning. Hercules got up and gave a testimony of God's grace, His unmerited favor, in sending Jesus to touch him. He told the congregation of how he had been blessed with a wonderful family and a business of his own. He told of how he had stopped attending church because he had become so caught up in his work. He said that he wasn't faithful in reading God's Word consistently, and he wondered why God would choose to save him from death. He was crying, and his broken English didn't make it any easier for him. His most fervent prayer, he said, was that he would never forget the love and grace God had shown to him.

Many people in the congregation were crying as well. Hercules left the platform slowly. His legs were shaking under the weight of his body. His weakened arms could barely keep the crutches at his side. The silence of the moment was broken by the sobs of the congregation.

Pastor Schroeder then asked the congregation if there was anyone who would like to commit himself to following the Lord Jesus Christ. He asked everyone to bow his head in a silent prayer and said that those who wished to make a decision should raise their hands. After the service, Dave told us that several people had made a commitment to the Lord that morning. Another victory.

Our Messiah, Jesus, has many names. Isaiah referred to Him as the Anointed Preacher, the Arm of the Lord, Divine Servant, Prince of Peace, Immanuel, only Savior. In John's gospel He is known as the Bread of Life, the Water of Life, Defender of the Weak, the Resurrection and the Life, the True Vine, the Giver of the Spirit, and the Great Intercessor. Throughout the New Testament, Jesus shows us His glory through His grace. His love is a cause for wonder and amazement.

When I think of the many times I have disappointed my Lord, I can point to an equal number of times in which He has forgiven me and taken me back. He knows that I am just a child learning to walk with the help of His steadying hand. Once in a while I run. Sometimes I have to sit still. Whenever I take my eyes off Jesus, though, I fall flat on my face. It is only through Christ that I will ever walk closer to the Father.

God does not want gifts or sacrifices from us out of fear or a guilty conscience. He wants them out of an attitude of love for Him.

I have no idea why God chose me to be His servant and follow Him. I only know that I will be eternally joyful and eternally grateful, whatever the cost.

And the Word became flesh and dwelt among us,

full of grace and truth; we have beheld his glory, glory as of the only Son from the Father. . . . And from his fullness have we all received, grace upon grace [John 1:14, 16].